Conversation-Starters for Working with
Children and Adolescents After Trauma

CONVERSATION-STARTERS FOR **WORKING** WITH **CHILDREN** AND **ADOLESCENTS** AFTER TRAUMA

Simple Cognitive and Arts-Based Activities

DAWN D'AMICO, LCSW, PHD

Jessica Kingsley Publishers
London and Philadelphia

First published in Great Britain in 2022 by Jessica Kingsley Publishers
An imprint of Hodder & Stoughton Ltd
An Hachette Company

1

A CIP catalogue record for this title is available from
the British Library and the Library of Congress

ISBN 978 1 78775 144 6
eISBN 978 1 78775 145 3

Printed and bound in Great Britain by TJ Books Limited

Jessica Kingsley Publishers' policy is to use papers that are natural,
renewable and recyclable products and made from wood grown in
sustainable forests. The logging and manufacturing processes are expected
to conform to the environmental regulations of the country of origin.

Jessica Kingsley Publishers
Carmelite House,
50 Victoria Embankment,
London, EC4Y 0DZ, UK

www.jkp.com

MIX
Paper from
responsible sources
FSC
www.fsc.org   FSC® C013056

To Dad, thank you for teaching me persistence, tenacity, and one step at a time. I love you.

ACKNOWLEDGMENTS

I want to acknowledge the many individuals, families, and institutions that have led to the creation of this book. Stephen and the entire team at JKP/Hachette, thank you for your support, feedback, and ongoing dialog. I especially would like to thank my family for their continued encouragement in my writing career, especially Michael, Agatha, and of course, Dad.

Finally, I will never be able to thank enough the children, adolescents, and families I have worked with for over a quarter of a century. You have allowed me into your life and shared your most difficult times. I am honored and profoundly grateful.

CONTENTS

PREFACE

Hello again, friends and colleagues,

Several years and books have passed since we last met. I am glad to find you here again, and for those of you who are new to my work, I welcome you. This book is about hope, courage, hard truth, resiliency, and joy. Yes, joy. Joy because each one of us who works with children and adolescents who have experienced trauma can see many amazing, sometimes even miraculous, changes in those we serve.

This work is arduous for the children and adolescents and for us, the helpers. I have created this book to provide additional tools to make the work just a bit more sustaining, creative, and hopefully, from time to time, a more relaxed way for all of us to approach these discussions. I purposefully created these to keep us all moving forward in a comforting way. Again, I have used the familiarity of supplies such as eco glitter, markers, glue, recycled pizza boxes, ribbon, etc. And, of course, this book is green. Everything we use can be recycled and repurposed. I rarely use poster boards now; rather, I have an overflowing closet of recycled cardboard from many kind people as well as ribbon, eco glitter, paint, and markers. A great time to gather these items is directly before summer break or back-to-school shopping. Many people will throw out half-used bottles of paint, glue, etc. Some say half-used but, in my mind, they are half-full. We do not need to add more to landfill, including the technology landfill. Except for printing out images, there is no technology involved; just us, or you and the child or adolescent.

As you know, this work is deeply personal, intimate, and susceptible. I admire you, your tenacity, and your willingness to place yourself into these egregious narratives to move children and adolescents towards health, wellbeing, and stability. Let us walk together lightly on the earth with energy, conviction, and solace that you are, indeed, impacting in a serious and profound way children and adolescents.

All my best, your colleague,

Dawn

INTRODUCTION

This book is designed to help clinicians, school psychologists, teachers, aid workers, and graduate students who are working with children and adolescents, aged 5–17, who have experienced trauma. There is an assumption that the individuals using this book will have a background knowledge and understanding of trauma. The issue of trauma continues to become more and prevalent. It requires continued new and progressive techniques for the children, adolescents, and families who are impacted as well as the individuals who are helping them.

Many children and adolescents who have experienced trauma are closed or withdrawn. The new techniques in this book allow children and adolescents to open up and communicate to receive the help they need. They allow for the individual to be present or mindful with the practitioner. Objects are used that we can all identify with. These items are "green," timeless materials that are easy to use and recycle. Remember the smell of markers, the feel of glue or paint, and the sparkle of eco glitter. These items are easy to find, such as stickers and recycled cardboard, they create a mini footprint with a low impact on the environment and they are accessible for everyone. That is what you will find here.

This book, like my previous book, is designed to support practitioners, who often become discouraged and burned out—not necessarily leaving the profession but no longer working with this particular population. The techniques in this book can help to restore a freshness and interest in the clinician, and alleviate some of the stress that clinicians experience in highly emotionally charged sessions.

This book is based on a quarter century of work with children and adolescents and their families. It has been written to provide new techniques, which are desperately needed as we see a rise in child sexual abuse, child pornography, child sex trafficking, and physical abuse and neglect. In 1994 and 1995, when I worked with the International Rescue Association and Chiang Mai University on child sex trafficking, it was a rare discussion outside of undeveloped countries compared with today. We are now becoming more aware of the prevalence of these issues, and this book supplies additional support for those impacted by these traumas.

All case studies in this book are anonymized. Working with such children and adolescents has been, and continues to be, both an honor and a privilege.

To my colleagues and students, here are new tools to help you help them.

USE OF THIS BOOK

This book is developmentally appropriate for children and adolescents aged 5–17.

All the tools can be used in both individual and group formats. Most can be completed in one session. They will help children and adolescents to open up and the clinician to gather information. The tools help children and allow for the building of positive feelings, safety, and coping.

As we know, many children and adolescents experience multiple traumas, and we recognize that some individuals may have gaps in memory due to abuse or neglect.

We all have a life story. We must embrace these stories in places where they can be supported, and healed in places where it hurts.

As everyone learns in different ways, there are different types of tool in this book to allow for the use of different senses for a fuller and deeper understanding and communication exchange.

All tools allow for self-expression for the individual and information gathering for the clinician. Hands-on tools are tactile in nature. They allow individuals to connect through the sense of touch. We will be using many recycled and found items here. Visual and verbal tools use sight and communication to collect information, receive a message, or learn a skill.

Try out different types of activities and determine which best suit the individual you are working with.

This book is easy to use. Simply choose an activity from either Part 1 'Coping' or Part 2 'Positive Thinking'. I have divided the book into these parts as many times when working with a child or adolescent they cannot move to positive thinking without first having some coping skills in place. Other times, children and adolescents may have some coping skills in place and are stuck in negative thought patterns; then we can jump into positive thinking tools. You will find a supply list and directions, including questions to help the clinician. Each tool is followed by two case studies representing a young child and an adolescent.

For the supply list, please use your imagination and remember to be "green."

Have on hand:

- recycled cardboard such as a pizza box

- glue

- washable paints

- finger paints

- markers, crayons and paint brushes

- eco glitter, bubbles

- synthetic feathers—never real feathers, unless you are lucky enough to find them

- construction paper

- poster board

- star stickers or stamp

- dominoes

- stuffed toy cat or dog

- list of feeling words

- stickers of happy, scared, or sad faces.

If you run out of certain supplies, you can supplement with others. Be creative.

Part 1

COPING

PLAYING WITH KITTENS OR PUPPIES

HANDS-ON

Purpose

To enable the child or adolescent to calm down and change their emotional state.

What you will need

* ★ A stuffed toy—kitten or puppy

Activity

Discuss with the child or adolescent the idea of remembering a time or imagining playing with a kitten or a puppy. Discuss what the fur feels like. Is it soft and warm? What does the kitten or the puppy sound like—does it purr or bark? What does it smell like?

After remembering or imagining being with the kitten or puppy, how does the child or adolescent feel? Are they happy, relaxed, joyful, or peaceful? What do they notice in their body? More energy or more relaxed? Have their feelings of anxiety subsided?

Case study: Child

Lena is a three-year-old who was referred after being removed from her foster home for neglect. Lena has been in foster care since birth.

The clinician asked Lena if she could imagine petting a kitten or a puppy. She stated that she had petted both. Lena shared that her foster mom had a dog, but the dog had to go because it was mean to the kids. Lena told the clinician that the dog was not mean to her, and she remembered sitting by the dog on the couch and watching TV. She reported hugging the dog around the neck and giving the dog kisses. It was fun for her, and comforting for her to be around the dog. She revealed that she missed the dog and another child who lived in the household with her. She did not miss her foster mom, who was mean to her.

This was a good beginning for Lena—she was able to talk about a time that she felt good, and about things that had occurred in the foster home.

Case study: Adolescent

Jason is a 12-year-old who was referred for fighting behaviors in school.

The clinician explained the Playing with Kittens or Puppies tool. Jason shared that he had not had the opportunity to play with either kittens or puppies, but that he had wanted a puppy since he was eight. His dad had told him that when the family had more time, they would adopt a puppy. Every year since then Jason had asked for a puppy. He revealed that for the last two years he had been paid to walk his neighbors' two dogs. Jason revealed that he probably would not be able to get a puppy until he was an adult, because his mom was too busy with work and the other children since his dad had moved out.

Jason and the clinician talked about how difficult it must have been since his dad had moved out of the home and how his life had changed. Jason discovered that he really did look forward to quiet time with the neighbors' dogs. He had been given the responsibility to unlock his neighbors' home and let the dogs into the fenced back yard. Sometimes he just sat in the sun with the dogs, played ball with them, or gave them a longer walk. One time his neighbors took him to the dog park with them and Jason met many people and dogs.

It appeared that Jason discovered he had another adult resource, in his neighbors.

PULLING UP WEEDS

HANDS-ON

Purpose

To help the child or adolescent identify and rid themselves of painful images.

What you will need

- ★ An image of a garden full of weeds

- ★ Markers

- ★ Stickers of different kinds of flowers

Activity

Ask the child or adolescent to view the image of a garden with many weeds. Discuss the idea that for a garden to be healthy, we must make room for beautiful things to grow. This requires identifying and pulling out weeds and replacing them with flowers or plants that we want.

Case study: Child

Raquel is a five-year-old who was referred due to sadness and difficulty socializing and making friends in school.

The clinician showed Raquel a photograph of a garden with straggly looking weeds and a photograph of a well-cared-for garden. Raquel pointed to the well-cared-for garden and said that this was the kind of garden that her grandmother had. And her grandmother's garden was even bigger. She revealed that her mom had a garden and Raquel used to play in it, but she no longer played in it because there was too much garbage in it.

When asked what had happened to the garden, Raquel revealed that her mom and dad had been yelling, and her dad ended up throwing nails and old things from the garage into her mom's garden. Raquel witnessed this.

This conversation provided much insight into Raquel's family life.

Case study: Adolescent

JP is a 17-year-old who was referred for truancy issues.

The clinician discussed the Pulling Up Weeds tool and showed JP the image of the weed-choked garden. JP scoffed at the image. He stated that his neighborhood looked like this garden. He became angry and shared that no one really cared in his neighborhood or, for that matter, in his life. So why should he care? He stated that it did not matter to anyone if he went to school or not, so he would rather hang out with older people or just stay at home and sleep in.

DOMINOES

HANDS-ON

Purpose

For the child or adolescent to learn how one thought can lead to another and another, and soon thoughts may be racing.

What you will need

★ A set of dominoes

Activity

Stand the dominoes up in two lines. Have the child or adolescent touch the first line and then watch how one domino hits another and another, and so forth, down the line, until the entire line falls.

Discuss with the child or adolescent how our thoughts can be like dominoes. We may have a sad thought or remember a frightening image, and that can lead to more sad thoughts and frightening images. Sometimes we can just keep having a flood of negative thoughts.

Case study: Child

Iam is a five-year-old who was referred for anger and acting out issues in his K–5 classroom. Iam's parents were divorcing. Up until this point Iam had been doing very well at school, socially and academically.

The clinician introduced Iam to the Dominoes tool. Iam enjoyed making the dominoes topple. He revealed that at home, when his parents argued, it was like a domino effect on the entire family. First one parent started to yell and then the other parent yelled and then the entire family was yelling, including Iam and his brother. Iam revealed that sometimes the dog would howl.

This was especially important information—the clinician now knew more about the dynamics within the family home. This could be explored and brought to the attention of the parents, who could then have a better understanding of how their behavior was impacting the entire family, and how Iam was learning and reacting due to what he was witnessing and experiencing.

Case study: Adolescent

Olivia is a 17-year-old who was referred for anxiety. Her anxiety had become so bad that at times she picked her skin until she bled. She frequently was not able to attend school due to her anxiety.

The clinician introduced Olivia to the Dominoes tool. Olivia understood the concept and quickly pushed both lines of dominoes over. She stated that her thoughts were like dominoes. Since last year she had noticed that she could start with a simple feeling of nervousness and then started to dwell on the feeling; she then found thoughts that made her nervous or even fearful, and her thoughts just continued down that path until she ended up having a panic attack.

NO EXIT MAZE 1

Purpose

To discover what actions the individual child or adolescent has tried to alleviate their emotional pain.

What you will need

★ A drawing of a maze with several dead ends

★ Pencil

Activity

Show the child or adolescent the drawing of the maze. Talk about the many different twists and turns within the maze, and how, after several attempts to find the way out, they had not been successful.

Case study: Child

Olsten is a 10-year-old who was referred for sadness and depression.

The clinician introduced Olsten to the No Exit Maze 1 tool. Olsten immediately identified with it. She stated that she felt like she and her family had tried many things to help her to "get over" or "get rid of" her sadness and depression, but to no avail. Olsten stated that she felt as though she was personally at a dead end as her father had told her that if "this" (therapy) didn't work, he didn't know what to do for her. This statement terrified Olsten as she felt like perhaps there was no hope for her.

Case study: Adolescent

Ava is a 14-year-old who was referred for issues of running away and then being placed back into a group home.

The clinician introduced Ava to the No Exit Maze 1 tool. Ava immediately stated that she felt she was at a dead end. She stated that she was angry and frustrated because she did not believe she would be released from the group home until she was 18. She further stated that, "No family want me." The belief that family members did not want her made her angry and she then reacted by running away.

MAZE WITH EXIT

HANDS-ON

Purpose

To demonstrate and reinforce for the child or adolescent that the situation may be exceedingly difficult, but that we need to keep trying to find a way out, a better way, or a solution.

What you will need

★ A picture of a maze with one or several ways out

★ Pencil

Activity

Show the picture of the maze to the child or adolescent. Explain that mazes can be confusing, and that many mazes have more than one way out. Work together to identify the different ways out.

Case study: Child

Noah is a nine-year-old who was referred for running away from his aunt's home, where he is currently placed.

The clinician explained the Maze with Exit tool to Noah. Noah stated that he "hates mazes" and sometimes he felt like he was in one. The clinician talked about Noah's multiple episodes of running away from his aunt's home, with the final episode ending very poorly, leaving Noah alone in the dark, in freezing conditions. Noah talked about trying to get to a better place or making things better somewhere else. He did not like his aunt's home as "she really does not want him there" and was too strict.

The clinician and Noah talked about other alternatives to

running away, such as perhaps asking his aunt to meet with them (Noah and the clinician) to talk about his concerns and what could be done immediately to stop him running away.

Case study: Adolescent

Elijah is a 16-year-old who was referred after he had been sus-pended from school for the second time in three months. This suspension was due to him threatening a teacher with a broom.

The clinician introduced Elijah to the Maze with Exit tool. Elijah shared that he often felt as though there was no way out of the problems in his own life. He was always in trouble, even when it was not his fault. Elijah shared that he had grabbed the broom on impulse after the teacher had, yet again, "slammed his mom" for not attending the parent–teacher conference. Elijah revealed that his mom was taking care of his maternal grandmother and was trying to "watch" his older brother who had recently been released from jail. Elijah felt that no one had time for him or even saw him anymore, and he did not know what to do. He became noticeably short-tempered when people criticized his mom, yet, at the same time, he was also very frustrated with her and did not know how to get her attention.

BARREL RIDER

VISUAL/VERBAL

Purpose

To identify issues that are difficult or scary for the child or adolescent to face.

What you will need

★ A photograph or a video clip of a child or adolescent barrel rider

Activity

Show the child or adolescent the photograph or the video clip. Talk about how thoughtful and how determined the rider must be to come close enough to the barrel to be able to pick up the flag.

Case study: Child

Alex is an eight-year-old who was referred for issues of sudden bedwetting.

The clinician explained the Barrel Rider tool to Alex. Alex shared that he was afraid of going back to his dad's home for overnight visits. He shared that in the past his dad would yell at him or ignore him. Several times his dad would smoke cigarettes while Alex was present, which brought on his asthma attacks.

This was an excellent opening conversation with Alex. The clinician and Alex were able to discover that in Alex's most recent visits, his dad was no longer smoking, and he had not been yelling. It was further discovered that maybe Alex's dad might be trying to change. Alex was able to share a lot of fear and apprehension surrounding these visits.

Case study: Adolescent

Eden is a 16-year-old who was referred for depression and anxiety and a recent suicide attempt.

The clinician introduced the Barrel Rider tool to Eden. Eden stated that she had tried many times to talk with her parents about her anxiety and depression. She had been very brave and approached the issue of wanting medication due to suicidal thoughts. Eden revealed that her parents did not believe in medication and felt that she just had to tough it out.

This was a great beginning for Eden and the clinician.

NO EXIT MAZE 2

Purpose

To help the child or adolescent recognize when they are ruminating or trying to find a solution over and over on their own.

What you will need

- ★ An image of a maze with no way out
- ★ Pencil

Activity

Share the image of the maze with the child or adolescent. They may want to try to find a way out of the maze. Let them attempt to do so. After they have tried or have decided that there is no way out, ask them about times when they have been ruminating or have tried repeatedly on their own to find a solution but have been unable to.

Case study: Child

Nova is a seven-year-old. Her sister and mother were recently incarcerated. She currently lives with her grandmother.

The clinician introduced Nova to the No Exit Maze 2 tool. Nova attempted the maze several times. When asked about the tool, Nova revealed that she had been trying to "undo" some of her behaviors that she was told had caused her mom and sister to be incarcerated. Nova revealed that a neighbor had found her roaming the halls of her apartment building on her own and in her pajamas. She had not known how to find the way back to her apartment. She believed that if she had stayed in the apartment, her mom and sister would not have been in trouble. Her sister even yelled that it was Nova's fault when the police arrived.

Case study: Adolescent

Hunter is a 14-year-old who was referred due to anxiety and picking behaviors.

The clinician introduced Hunter to the No Exit Maze 2 tool. Hunter could see that there was no way out of the maze, and revealed that it felt as though there was no way out of his anxiety. He shared that he had seen numerous doctors and had been on different medications, but the feelings and thoughts kept going around in his head.

This was a great beginning for Hunter.

OBSERVING BUTTERFLIES

VISUAL/VERBAL

Purpose

To help the child or adolescent identify interesting and fun things around them.

What you will need

★ Images of butterflies

Activity

Share the images of the butterflies with the child or adolescent. Talk about all the different types, and discuss the different environments they are in. What are interesting or fun people or things the child or adolescent can identify within their own environment?

Case study: Child

Josiah is a seven-year-old who was referred for reactive attachment disorder.

The clinician explained the Observing Butterflies tool to Josiah. Josiah revealed that it was difficult for him to find fun things to think about or even talk about because he was always getting into trouble. He shared that his father called him "a bad kid." After talking about the "bad" things, Josiah shared that he was extremely interested in his father's rock collection, and that sometimes his father would sit down with him and tell him about it. They would hold and examine the rocks together.

This was a great beginning for Josiah and the clinician.

Case study: Adolescent

Avery is a 15-year-old who was referred for issues of trauma related to sexual abuse by a family member.

The clinician introduced Avery to the Observing Butterflies tool. Avery talked about her particular interest in Blue Morpho butterflies. She revealed that she hoped to be able to take the school trip to South America to see these butterflies. After discussing her keen interest in butterflies, Avery was able to talk about other things that interested her and that were fun for her to explore. She recognized that she did not have to always think or "feel" the trauma to process it. She could have fun breaks and follow her interests.

BUTTERFLY BUSH

VISUAL/VERBAL

Purpose

To help the child or adolescent cope and recognize that many people are trying to work towards the same goal, by visualizing something fun and warm and alive with activity.

What you will need

★ An image of a butterfly bush with many butterflies landing on it and/or flying around it

Activity

Show the child or the adolescent the image of the busyness of the butterfly bush. Discuss the activity, and how alive the bush is with butterflies. Note the different types of butterflies all working towards the same purpose—to gather nectar.

Case study: Child

Anastasia is an 11-year-old who was referred due to the trauma of her father's suicide.

The clinician introduced Anastasia to the Butterfly Bush tool. Anastasia was initially interested, and then she started to cry. She revealed that her mother, brother, grandmother, and many others were all trying to work towards the same goal, which was trying to understand why her father had committed suicide. Anastasia was able to express great grief, fear, and frustration. It appeared to her as though everyone was trying in their own way, but they were not working together. Her mom stayed in her bedroom, "most of the day," and she couldn't talk with her paternal grandparents who lived nearby because she didn't want to cause them to cry, "again."

Case study: Adolescent

Chantelle is a 16-year-old who was referred due to the trauma of her mother's incarceration.

The clinician introduced Chantelle to the Butterfly Bush tool. Chantelle was able to readily identify that before her mother's incarceration she felt that many people were working towards helping her mother and helping Chantelle to graduate high school. Chantelle revealed that now that her mother had been incarcerated it felt like everyone had abandoned her or given up on her due to her mother's behavior. This tool helped Chantelle to get to core beliefs and needs very quickly so that she could get the assistance she needed during this tumultuous time.

WHAT DOES THE HEART NEED NOW?

Purpose

To determine what the child or adolescent needs to help make them feel happy or safe or at peace.

What you will need

- ★ Paint or markers
- ★ Paintbrushes
- ★ Recycled paper

Activity

Give the child or adolescent the opportunity to paint or draw a representation of their heart. Encourage them to create a large heart, as big as the paper that you provide.

Ask the child or adolescent, what does their heart tell them that they need right now? Discuss the difference between "wants" and "needs." Help them to determine what would help them to feel happy or safe or at peace. Could they ask someone for help? What one step could the child or adolescent take to get what they need?

Case study: Child

Sam is an 11-year-old who was referred for issues of reactive attachment disorder.

The clinician introduced Sam to the What Does the Heart Need Now? tool. Sam painted his heart—large and vibrant. He shared that he needed more time with his father. He felt alone and isolated from him.

Case study: Adolescent

Gianna is a 16-year-old who was referred for testing positive for sexually transmitted diseases for the fourth time this year.

The clinician introduced Gianna to the What Does the Heart Need Now? tool. Gianna stated that she needed her life to settle down. She was experiencing wild and disconcerting shifts in her emotional state. She revealed that she had had several panic attacks and multiple sleepless nights, since it seemed she continued to "sleep with jerks."

This information allowed the clinician to streamline services to help Gianna to take positive steps to understanding sexually contracted diseases, to protect herself, and overall, to take better care of herself.

SOMETHING BEAUTIFUL

VISUAL/VERBAL

Purpose

To help the child or adolescent calm down, slow down, and get quiet, as a temporary respite from worry.

What you will need

★ Several images of beautiful things, such as a sunset, a rose, or whatever else you would like

Activity

Show the child or adolescent the images and ask them which they find to be the most beautiful. Ask them to take a couple of deep breaths with you, and to just gaze at the image for several seconds. Ask them to close their eyes and to imagine the image.

Ask if they can notice their body calming down or getting quiet. Remind them how simply they can step out of a worry state, even for a couple of minutes, by practicing this tool.

Case study: Child

Lachian is an eight-year-old who was referred for childhood diabetes.

The clinician explained the Something Beautiful tool to Lachian. Lachian responded that he felt shy or embarrassed to talk about beautiful things because he felt so ugly. He further revealed in this initial meeting that he was being bullied due to his weight issues.

This initial conversation allowed the clinician to learn very quickly several obstacles that Lachian was encountering. Lachian talked about his concerns and was then able to try the tool and feel less troubled and calmer.

Case study: Adolescent

Charlotte is a 15-year-old who was recently released from a teen detention center for physical violence against others.

The clinician explained the Something Beautiful tool to Charlotte. Charlotte stated that there were not many beautiful things in the world. She revealed that she was angry with her parents, "the system," her case manager, and many others for placing her in a detention center. She revealed that she "was not that bad." She shared her various experiences and was quite agitated. It was decided to end the conversation by focusing on the image of the rose that she had chosen.

The tool helped Charlotte to calm down and to literally feel a change in her body, a release of tension.

HOLDING ON

VISUAL/VERBAL

Purpose

To determine what thought or feeling the child or adolescent cannot let go of or get past.

What you will need

★ Only you

Activity

Share the idea that even though the child or adolescent has moved forward in their life after a crisis, sometimes feelings are memories that just keep coming back, as if we cannot let go of them or cannot get away from them.

Case study: Child

Lily is a 10-year-old who was referred for continued feelings of sadness and anger after she was reunited with her mother.

The clinician introduced Lily to the Holding On tool. Lily readily revealed that she had ongoing feelings of distress, including fear, sadness, and worry. She kept remembering when her mom had left the home and did not return. For a period, her grandmother cared for her. Now her mom and her grandmother cared for her. She revealed that she loved her mom but was fearful that her mom might leave again and may never return.

Case study: Adolescent

Xavier is a 15-year-old who was referred for vandalism and attempted arson of a school mate's car.

Xavier was introduced to the Holding On tool and was reactive. He raised his voice and boasted about his actions. He stated that it was nothing and was stuck on the idea that he would retaliate against his enemies. He further stated that he was happy that people at school knew what had happened.

This beginning conversation was revealing of Xavier's emotional state, the issue of enemies, and the need for him to strike out.

A FRESH START

VISUAL/VERBAL

Purpose

For the child or adolescent to be able to identify alternatives and what they can do.

What you will need

★ Only you

Activity

Ask the child or adolescent to imagine a brand-new opportunity. What would it look like? What would they be doing? Where would they live? Who would be in their life?

Case study: Child

Jackson is a nine-year-old who was referred for adjustment issues after starting a new school.

The clinician introduced Jackson to the A Fresh Start tool. Jackson identified that one fresh start would be that his mom would not have been relocated for her job so that he could stay at the same school. He revealed that he had not been very friendly and had pushed several potential friends away. He was not sure if his teacher liked him either.

This was a great beginning to opening up for Jackson.

Case study: Adolescent

Blake is 17-year-old who was referred for truancy, drug use, and failing grades in his senior year.

The clinician introduced Blake to the A Fresh Start tool. Blake revealed that he wished that he could start his senior year of high school over. He would change many of his behaviors. Blake was able to identify that he had been spending a lot of time with his cousin, who had moved into his home. His cousin was older, had dropped out of school, and had supplied Blake with marijuana. Blake revealed that he was afraid of his cousin, who he believed might be involved in a gang. He was fearful that if he did not do what his cousin wanted, his cousin could hurt him.

BE PATIENT

VISUAL/VERBAL

Purpose

For the child or adolescent to learn to be patient and kind to themselves when learning new skills.

What you will need

★ Only you

Activity

Ask the child or adolescent to think about and imagine how they would feel towards a toddler or a kitten or a puppy learning a new skill. How would they show kindness, gentleness, and patience? Can they apply these behaviors of kindness, gentleness, and patience towards themselves? How? What is one step that they could take today?

Case study: Child

Dreamer is a five-year-old who was referred for daytime wetting issues. As punishment, Dreamer's parents make her wear diapers or pull-ups, even though she has been toilet-trained since the age of two.

The clinician introduced Dreamer to the Be Patient tool. Dreamer started to cry and said she was trying her best, but that her parents yelled at her. Dreamer shared that at school she was afraid to ask to go to the bathroom as she had seen her teacher become impatient when other students asked. She also believed that her teacher would tell her that she could not go.

Dreamer also revealed that at home her parents yelled at her and at each other, and when that happened, she felt the urgency to urinate but could not make it to the bathroom on time. This helped the clinician understand what was happening in the various environments that cause distress for Dreamer. This also allowed for the clinician to better educate Dreamer's parents and her teacher.

Case study: Adolescent

Tahlia is a 17-year-old who was referred for trichotillomania. She has a history of pulling out the hair on her head.

The clinician introduced Tahlia to the Be Patient tool. Tahlia was initially apprehensive about discussing her trichotillomania; however, she revealed that when she became anxious about school, homework, or her friends, she started to pull out her hair. She also revealed that lately she had been pulling out her eyebrows and her eyelashes too. Tahlia revealed that this had happened before, and she had been able to stop the behaviors by using a variety of techniques, especially journaling. She attempted the journaling again, but it did not work for her, and she had reverted to calling herself names and pulling more of her hair out.

The clinician reinforced the idea that Tahlia had coped with this condition in the past, and together they explored several coping techniques. The focus, however, returned to the idea of being patient and gentle, and recognizing that learning new techniques and implementing old techniques takes time and may take multiple efforts.

Tahlia agreed to be more patient and kinder to herself, and to monitor and change her negative self-talk.

GRATITUDE

VISUAL/VERBAL

Purpose

To help the child or adolescent recall and recreate good, positive experiences.

What you will need

★ Only you

Activity

Introduce the child or adolescent to simple gratitude questions. Have them recall what they experienced and how they felt. Take the next step of getting them to think about what they could do today to recreate the feeling of gratitude.

> What is one thing that they have done for someone else that they are happy or grateful that they did? What is one thing that they did for themselves that they are happy or grateful for? Can they think about something that they could do today—just one thing, no matter how small—that they could do for themselves or for another person that could make them happy or grateful today?

Case study: Child

Lisa is an eight-year-old who was referred following the death of her mother due to cancer.

The clinician introduced Lisa to the Gratitude tool. Lisa was quick to remember and proudly recite the many times when she had helped her mom, and made her mom's day brighter by giving her cards or simply snuggling with her in bed. Lisa was proud of and grateful for her actions. Lisa recognized that she needed to do something today to help make herself feel happy or good. She decided to draw a picture of her mom, and to ask her grandmother for a photograph of her mom when she was Lisa's age.

Case study: Adolescent

Michelle is a 17-year-old who was referred for ongoing issues of depression and anxiety.

The clinician introduced Michelle to the Gratitude tool. At first Michelle said that she was so depressed and anxious that she couldn't think of anything that she was grateful for. After a bit of discussion, she revealed that she felt grateful for spending time in the sunshine. She revealed that on days when she had little motivation, she could at least sit in the sunshine with her mom. Sometimes her mom would bring lunch outside and they would eat together, although many times Michelle lacked an appetite.

Michelle decided that today she would do what worked for her, which was to sit in the sunshine and to make lunch for her mom.

QUIET, SAFE, CALM, OR RELAXED

HANDS-ON

Purpose

To help the child or adolescent feel quiet, safe, calm, or relaxed.

What you will need

- ★ Paper

- ★ Markers or crayons

- ★ Magazines

Activity

Ask the child or adolescent if they have a place where they can go where they feel safe and peaceful—perhaps a quiet nook in their house or apartment, or a special park. If they are unable to think of a real place, ask them to choose an image from a magazine where they can imagine being. With all the noise of our everyday life, both inside and outside, ask them to draw one place that they can go to in their mind's eye that can make them feel quiet, safe, calm, or relaxed.

Case study: Child

Lexi is a five-year-old who was referred for issues over family reunification.

The clinician explained the Quiet, Safe, Calm, or Relaxed activity to Lexi, the idea of drawing a place that is quiet or safe or peaceful. Lexi was able to draw a house on a lake. It was the place where she and her extended family went for weekends and holidays in the summer.

Case study: Adolescent

Josh is a 17-year-old who was referred for transitioning to his married older brother's home after being in the foster care system for the last few years.

The clinician introduced Josh to the Quiet, Safe, Calm, or Relaxed tool. Josh was able to immediately identify with it—he is a talented artist. He drew a large oblong table full of people. He shared that this was what dinnertime was like at his brother's house. There were multiple children, his sisters-in-law, and parents, whom he liked, and "everyone eats together." Josh expressed that he could not wait to be permanently with his brother. He felt consistency and safety, calm, and love in this environment. He also shared that he had never felt that way before.

STEP BACK, TURN AWAY FROM PAIN

HANDS-ON

Purpose

To help the child or adolescent cope with pain, and to work out the first step they can take to turn away from the pain.

What you will need

- ★ Lined paper
- ★ Pen or pencil
- ★ Brightly colored star stickers or stamps

Activity

Ask the child or adolescent to explore ways with you that would enable them to move away physically or emotionally from pain. Create a list that they can keep and use when needed. Star or stamp the activities that could be the easiest for them to initiate.

Case study: Child

Mimi is a five-year-old who misses her father and mother, both of whom have been incarcerated.

The clinician explained the Step Back, Turn Away from Pain tool. Mimi proudly showed a tiny stuffed dog she had in her pocket, which she carried every day. Her mom gave it to her before she left, and when she held the dog, it reminded her of her mom. The smell of the stuffed animal reminded her of home.

Mimi already had ways of coping and self-comforting and

turning away from pain. We explored several more to place on her list. She used crayons to create drawings of her aunt, her teacher at school, and her favorite book. The clinician wrote the words next to the drawings. Together they placed the stars next to the items that were the easiest for her to carry out.

Case study: Adolescent

Harmony is a 16-year-old who was referred for issues of anxiety and trichotillomania. She pulls her hair out in clumps from her head, and she has bald spots and bleeding. She has recently also been pulling out her eyebrows and eyelashes. She is currently being treated for a recent infection in one of her eyelids.

The clinician introduced Harmony to the Step Back, Turn Away from Pain tool. Harmony and the clinician had worked together on coping with her anxiety and trichotillomania. Harmony revealed that she was ashamed and embarrassed as she had a period where she had had these issues under control. Harmony revealed that she would be graduating from high school at the age of 17, and was overly concerned about what would happen next. She had college applications, and her family could not help her, and did not seem interested. She revealed that she was feeling overwhelmed.

Together the clinician and Harmony created a list of actions that she could undertake to help with her anxiety and depression. Some of the actions included reconnecting with her high school counselor, who had been critical in helping Harmony to negotiate getting ready to graduate early and going to college.

Other actions on the list included: not playing with her hair, which she stated usually led to her pulling it; wearing a ponytail; and using a simple technique such as a rubber band or bracelet that she could gently snap instead of her hair-pulling behavior.

Finally, she decided to take out her journal again and write her thoughts down in it to avoid her continued ruminations. Harmony placed stamps on every item on the list, including one on her hand.

TRUST

Purpose

To help the child or adolescent identify individuals in the environment who are safe and readily available to them.

What you will need

- ★ Paper
- ★ Pens or crayons

Activity

Create a list of safe people and places with the child or adolescent. These are people and places that they can trust, and that will be stable, accessible, and present, if needed.

Case study: Child

Kasha is a five-year-old who was referred for possible attachment issues. Kasha had been adopted by Filipino family members who lived in England. They then relocated to the US due to a job promotion. Kasha was doing well prior to this second relocation. After moving to the US, the family struggled to find a Filipino church and community, which, in the past, had seemed to help the entire family, especially Kasha, who was surrounded by native speakers and children at community and church events.

The clinician explained the Trust tool to Kasha. Kasha stated that she could trust her adoptive mom and her grandma (who lived in the Philippines). She was not sure at this point who else she could trust or rely on, as everything had changed. She really struggled with the language, and cried about not understanding or being able to read as well as others in her grade.

Kasha and the clinician decided they would share with her adoptive mom her concerns and how much she really relied on her.

Case study: Adolescent

Daniel is a 13-year-old who was referred for suicidal ideation, depression, and anxiety.

The clinician introduced Daniel to the Trust tool. Daniel shared that he did have people he could trust. He believed that his core group of friends and his best friend had saved his life several times. He shared that his best friend had called his parents and told his teacher when Daniel needed help. Daniel also trusted his parents and his older sister.

Daniel tried to trust the medications that he was on, but sometimes they made him feel sick. Daniel talked about speaking with his psychiatrist to let her know that he was having these feelings of nausea. Daniel discovered that he had many people he could trust and who were resources in his life.

ON TRACK OR LOST

VISUAL/VERBAL

Purpose

To help the child or adolescent get back on track, moving in a healthy and solution-focused direction. To help them work out which track they are on now, and who helps them to stay on track or get back on track.

What you will need

★ Only you

Activity

Introduce the child or adolescent to the idea of staying on track, doing what they need to do to feel healthy, purposeful, and/or safe and calm. Sometimes it seems like we are on track and doing the right thing, moving in the direction that we need to be going. We feel happy or have more energy. Other times we feel like we are lost, and we do not know which way to go. We feel fear or anger or sadness. Ask the child or adolescent for some beginning ideas for getting back on track.

Case study: Child

Kennan is a 10-year-old who was referred for child-on-child sexual touching at school.

The clinician explained the On Track or Lost tool to Kennan. Kennan revealed that he had felt immense embarrassment with his family and friends. He felt as though he had been on track before the incident at school happened. He was getting ready to move into middle school, but his parents relocated him to a different school mid-semester. It was a private school, so he would most likely not see the friends he had grown up with again. Kennan revealed that his older cousin had sexually touched him earlier this year.

Case study: Adolescent

Mica is a 17-year-old who was referred for issues of anger and truancy.

The clinician introduced Mica to the On Track or Lost tool. Mica stated that he was off track. He had worked with the clinician previously and had been able to control his anger issues and his truancy behaviors. He stated that ever since starting his senior year of high school he had returned to his old group of friends, who he felt more comfortable with. This group encouraged him to drink alcohol, smoke, and skip school. At this point he felt like he was lost. He was angry. He knew that college wasn't for him, but he wasn't sure what to do next. Many of his friends from a healthier friendship group had jobs, or had gone to college or technical school, or were on internship plans.

Mica decided to follow up with his school counselor, who arranged for career testing to occur, although Mica skipped school on the day of the last testing appointment. He now plans to take the test and to see what some of his strengths and options are, to get back on track.

SAFE HEART

HANDS-ON

Purpose

To determine what needs to be in place for the child or adolescent to feel safe again.

What you will need

- ★ A large heart made from construction paper
- ★ Markers
- ★ Eco glitter
- ★ Star stickers

Activity

Share with the child or adolescent the heart made from construction paper. Ask them to think and feel from their heart about what they need to feel safe. Create a list of resources they can use, including people, places, and things. They can decorate the heart with eco glitter and star stickers.

Case study: Child

Sammie is a 10-year-old who was referred for trauma after being sexually abused by her brother.

The clinician introduced Sammie to the Safe Heart tool. Sammie stated that even though her brother was no longer in the home, she continued to feel unsafe, and specifically at home. Sammie listed many people who would help her to feel safe, including her parents, aunt, sisters, and cousins. One of the interesting things that was discovered in Sammie's list is that she wanted a lock on her bedroom door and on the bathroom door. Sammie revealed that the locks had been taken off due to Sammie locking herself in the bathroom and her parents being fearful for her safety.

This was a great beginning for Sammie.

Case study: Adolescent

David is a 17-year-old who was referred for issues of anxiety due to moving on to college and away from his mother.

The clinician introduced David to the Safe Heart tool. David revealed that his mother was an active alcoholic, and he was concerned that when he left for college, she would die. This tool allowed David to demonstrate the severity of his concern for his mother and his willingness to forgo continuing education to help her.

This was a great opening up for David.

THE WORLD OUTSIDE OF YOU

Purpose

To help the child or adolescent move from being focused on the trauma to having time where they can think about the largeness, beauty, and interesting things in the world.

What you will need

- ★ Images of deep-sea divers, rockets, nature, etc.
- ★ Images from your own areas of interest
- ★ Poster board or pizza box
- ★ Glue
- ★ Safety scissors

Activity

Share with the child or adolescent the richness of the world and that this tool is about thinking outside of our scope of reference right now, giving ourselves a break from the trauma. Share some of the images that you have collected. If you feel comfortable, include images from your own areas of interest, for example from animals to spider web photography. After reviewing the various images, create together a list of interesting things in the world, be they other beings, places, plants, etc. They can cut out and glue images onto the poster board or pizza box. Is there an opportunity for the child or adolescent to learn more about the topics of their choice through the library or other people? Explore the options.

Case study: Child

Savannah is a seven-year-old who was referred after relocating with her family to a different State.

The clinician introduced Savannah to The World Outside of You tool. Savannah revealed that everything was so different currently. Her mom and dad were busy working in their new jobs, and usually the summer would be an adventure with her friends. This summer, if she had continued living at her old home, Savannah would have gone on a high adventure summer camp, with snorkeling and horseback riding, etc. Savannah revealed that she had never been on a horse and now that they were no longer living near the ocean, she most likely would not be able to snorkel. The clinician shared that plenty of horse stables existed locally, and although she might not be able to snorkel in the sea, maybe she could snorkel in the various lakes nearby? Savannah also expressed an interest in spider web photography—she was interested in seeing more spider webs at the nearby parks.

This was a good beginning for Savannah to explore and expand her options.

Case study: Adolescent

Ernesto is a 17-year-old who was referred after his twin brother was diagnosed with kidney disease.

The clinician introduced Ernesto to The World Outside of You tool. Ernesto shared that it was exceedingly difficult for him to think of anything right now other than his brother. He was a perfect match to provide his brother with a kidney replacement, and at the same time there was an ongoing fear that he may eventually have kidney disease himself. Before the diagnosis Ernesto was looking at colleges, and spending time with his girlfriend and his brother. The image of the deep-sea diver reminded Ernesto that they had all planned on taking a trip to Mexico after high school. They wanted to snorkel, handglide, and see the Aztec ruins.

The clinician and Ernesto talked about taking breaks to be

able to relax and regain perspective on this big decision. Ernesto was quite sure he would donate his kidney to his brother. He also shared that they could then all plan for the vacation. It was not when they had planned to do it, and indeed, he might not be able to start college in the Fall, but these were all things that he could sort out together with his family.

WHAT DO WE DO WHEN WE GET SCARED?

HANDS-ON

Purpose

To provide the child or adolescent with coping tools, to help them reach out for help.

What you will need

- ★ Paper
- ★ Pen

Activity

Ask the child or adolescent to create a list of coping behaviors that they already engage in, and a second list of individuals who are readily accessible that the child or adolescent can reach out to for help or reassurance. Reinforce the idea that the child or adolescent already has a coping skill set and individuals who are available to help them.

Case study: Child

Kasia is a 10-year-old who was referred for recent issues of hiding food, purposefully urinating on the floor, and lying to her mother and her teacher.

The clinician introduced Kasia to the What Do We Do When We Get Scared? tool. Kasia struggled to create a list of healthy coping techniques, but she was able to identify her mother, her aunt, and her two older sisters as individuals who were available to help.

This was a good beginning as Kasia identified that she did not have a healthy set of coping tools and was using food as a way of coping. Further, she identified feelings of overwhelming anger at times.

Case study: Adolescent

Cody is a 17-year-old who was referred for ongoing truancy issues that may delay his graduation from high school. He is also involved in a criminal court case.

The clinician introduced Cody to the What Do We Do When We Get Scared? tool. Cody stated that he did not feel fearful about anything, and therefore did not need any coping skills. Cody further shared that he had plenty of support and people he could identify who would help him. The clinician noted that his entire list consisted of his friends, some of whom were involved in the criminal court case. With further discussion, Cody alluded to his group being a gang.

This tool allowed the clinician to gather critical information including the lack of support that Cody was getting, potential gang affiliation and activity, and finally, a beginning into understanding Cody's anger.

WHO OR WHAT IS HOLDING YOU BACK?

HANDS-ON

Purpose

To gain information about significant stressors in the child's or adolescent's life.

What you will need

* ★ Paper
* ★ Pen

Activity

Ask the child or adolescent to create a list of feelings or people or events they feel are holding them back or impeding them from obtaining a goal or moving forward.

Case study: Child

Asher is an 11-year-old who was referred for issues of sadness and anger after his parents divorced.

The clinician introduced Asher to the Who or What Is Holding You Back? tool. Asher stated that he felt significant confusion and stress over his parents' rules and thoughts surrounding religion. His mom and dad had raised him in one religion and now, since his parents' divorce, his mom had changed religions. He felt very confused and frustrated. He revealed that he believed that his dad was doing the right thing and that his mom was attempting to change the beliefs he had held since he could remember.

This tool was especially useful for the clinician as, until the discovery of the religious issue, everyone thought the issue was about his parents arguing.

Case study: Adolescent

Mila is a 15-year-old who was referred for anxiety and depression, which has become worse over the school year.

The clinician introduced Mila to the Who or What Is Holding You Back? tool. Mila was able to share that she was holding herself back. She revealed that she found herself comparing and judging herself against her peers. The more she found herself to be less "perfect" than her peers, the harder she worked.

This was a useful tool as the clinician was able to identify an increasing move towards perfectionism over time for Mila with her school performance.

SPIRAL: COME BACK TO CENTER

HANDS-ON

Purpose

To identify a trigger event or stressor that has caused ongoing distress for the child or adolescent.

What you will need

★ An image of a spiral that is large enough to be written on, this can be a hand drawn image

★ Pens or markers

Activity

Ask the child or adolescent to identify feelings that were generated by a particularly stressful event. Place the event in the middle of the spiral and notate feelings and other symptoms of distress throughout the spiral. Check for a change in their worldview.

Case study: Child

Leo is a 10-year-old who was referred for issues of night terrors and bedwetting.

The clinician introduced Leo to the Spiral: Come Back to Center tool. Leo was able to identify several events that could be considered major stressors, including his parents' drug use, his father's recent release from prison, and several moves to different homes and schools. Further, Leo was able to identify symptoms of nausea, diarrhea, headaches, difficulty sleeping, sadness, rage, and more.

This was an excellent beginning discussion for Leo. The clinician was able to identify numerous stressors as well as symptoms that Leo was able to discuss.

Case study: Adolescent

Vivian is a 16-year-old who was referred after revealing a classmate had sexually assaulted her.

The clinician explained the Spiral: Come Back to Center tool to Vivian. Vivian was immediately able to relate to the tool and could identify multiple symptoms of trauma resulting in a change of her worldview—the world being unsafe, and that people were untrustworthy.

The tool helped the clinician to quickly assess Vivian's symptoms from the beginning to the change of her worldview.

CREATE WITH YOUR HEART

Purpose

To create a sense of soothing and calm for the child or adolescent, using color and paint.

What you will need

- ★ Finger paints
- ★ Poster board or recycled cardboard

Activity

Ask the child or adolescent to choose a color or colors that most represent(s) their heart. Ask them to use their fingers to paint— encourage a real tactile experience.

Case study: Child

Mateo is a nine-year-old who was referred for issues of grief after the death of his grandmother, whom he had grown up with in the family home.

The clinician introduced Mateo to the Create with Your Heart tool. Mateo hesitantly dipped his fingers in the paint. He laughed and said that it was cold. He smelled the paint and said it smelled like grapes. Mateo used one finger to paint an image of him and his grandmother holding hands while standing among flowers. He chose many colors for the flowers, and shared a peace-filled memory of helping his grandmother in her garden.

This tool was helpful for the clinician to help Mateo cope and self-soothe with his good memories of his grandmother.

Case study: Adolescent

Eliana is a 17-year-old who was referred for issues of stress and anxiety.

The clinician introduced Eliana to the Create with Your Heart tool. Eliana poured paint into her hand and used her entire hand to layer on light-blue swaths of color, taking up virtually the entire poster board. Eliana revealed that she loved to paint and used to paint frequently until the stressors of school became so difficult that she no longer had the time or the patience for her artwork.

The tool helped the clinician to quickly identify one way of self-soothing for Eliana, and that, historically, creating art, and in particular painting, had been something Eliana had experienced as joyful and empowering.

WASH AWAY PAIN

HANDS-ON

Purpose

To help the child or adolescent articulate their pain, and begin to process through it.

What you will need

- ★ Large poster board with the image of a bathtub filled with soap bubbles stuck on it
- ★ Stick-on drawings of soap bubbles
- ★ Markers

Activity

Discuss with the child or adolescent that the soap bubbles represent painful feelings that need to be addressed and then let go of or washed away. Ask the child or adolescent to fill in the stick-on bubbles with painful memories or events.

Ask about what it would feel like after all the soap bubbles have been washed away, or all the painful events have been removed.

Case study: Child

Hugo is a 10-year-old who was referred for feelings of sadness and irritability.

The clinician discussed with Hugo the Wash Away Pain tool. Hugo was tearful as he wrote down the names of his paternal grandparents. He also drew a heart with a thunderbolt through it. Hugo shared his feelings of sadness, anger, and fear. He revealed that his grandparents had returned to Mexico and he did not know when he would see them again. Hugo had a close bond with both his grandmother and grandfather as he had lived with them in Mexico until about two years ago. Hugo could imagine the pain and longing for his grandparents going away, but only when they returned.

This tool was helpful to swiftly move Hugo into a discussion of painful issues.

Case study: Adolescent

Roxanne is a 15-year-old who was referred for alcohol and other drug issues. She has been suspended from school for possession of alcohol and marijuana.

The clinician explained the Wash Away Pain tool to Roxanne. Roxanne placed the name of her boyfriend, her best friend, and her mom in the stick-on soap bubbles. Roxanne explained that her life was complicated and that her mom was overprotective and would not allow Roxanne as many privileges and freedoms as her peers. She revealed that it was common for "everyone" to be high or intoxicated at school.

This tool allowed a discussion to begin about the difficult issue of alcohol and drug use among minors.

BUBBLE-POP

HANDS-ON

Purpose

To demonstrate to the child or adolescent in a fun way the impermanence of feelings states for increased coping.

What you will need

★ Bubbles

Activity

Blow bubbles together with the child or adolescent then read out the following script:

> As bubbles move away into the sky or the room, watch them pop and disappear. Imagine what it would feel like just for a moment for all our internal strife or concerning feelings states to disappear.

Case study: Child

Sawyer is an 11-year-old who was referred for issues of anxiety and picking her skin until she causes it to bleed.

The clinician explained the Bubble-Pop tool to Sawyer. Sawyer and the clinician blew bubbles together. Sawyer revealed that she wished that her fear would just go away, but every time she thought it had gone, it reappeared. Sawyer revealed that her mom and dad had repeated arguments and shouted at each other about divorce. At times, the arguing stopped, but then it inevitably returned.

This tool helped the clinician to move to the root of Sawyer's concerns in a timely manner.

Case study: Adolescent

Tia is a 16-year-old who was referred for issues of anxiety.

The clinician introduced Tia to the Bubble-Pop tool. Tia revealed that she experienced anxiety, that it went away and then it came back. She shared that she was unable to determine the source of the anxiety and it kept reoccurring.

This was a great opening for Tia.

ILLUMINATE OR LIGHT YOUR PATH

VISUAL/VERBAL

Purpose

To identify who or what helps the child or adolescent to move from darkness into light.

What you will need

★ Images of one walking path that is light and one that is dark

Activity

Show the child or adolescent both images, of the light walking path and the dark walking path. Ask them to identify which one feels better.

Sometimes we need to ask for help from others to light the way, to make it clear and safe to move forward, and sometimes we need to be the light for ourselves. Ask the child or adolescent, what do they need right now to help them find their way, to move from darkness into light?

Case study: Child

Samuel is an eight-year-old who was referred for help with his autism spectrum disorder. He has recently been acting out towards his mother and stepfather. He has also name-called his mother.

The clinician introduced Samuel to the Illuminate or Light Your Path tool. Samuel shared that he frequently felt as though he must light his own path and educate others. He shared feelings of embarrassment regarding his mother and stepfather, as he said he knew more about science than both of them. He also revealed some anger regarding his mother's and stepfather's inability to help him in some areas of his homework.

This tool allowed Samuel to communicate strong feelings about his mother and stepfather as well as his own self-perception.

Case study: Adolescent

Kiki is a 14-year-old who was referred for issues of acting out in school, including name-calling, bullying, and incivility.

The clinician explained the Illuminate or Light Your Path tool to Kiki. Kiki stated that she did not need anyone to light her path; in fact, she felt better on her own in the darkness.

This information allowed the clinician to discuss with Kiki the darkness and the alone times, and the issues that had brought her there.

LADYBUG

HANDS-ON

Purpose

To help the child or adolescent identify issues (or spots) in their lives that need strengthening.

What you will need

- ★ A large picture or drawing of a ladybug that can be colored in
- ★ Black marker
- ★ Crayons

Activity

Share with the child or adolescent the image of the ladybug. Ask them to imagine that the dots on the ladybug's back represent areas in their life where they need help or that need strengthening.

Case study: Child

Anita is an eight-year-old who was referred for issues of night terrors. Anita had found her mother unconscious due to alcohol and drug usage.

The clinician introduced Anita to the Ladybug tool. Anita started coloring the image of the ladybug. She stated that she used to find ladybugs in the garden. She started to cry and shared that she had been fearful for her mom. She was worried that her mom would die, and thought that when her mom was unconscious she was dead.

The clinician and Anita filled in the dots together with nightmares, mom's "sickness," fear, and sadness.

Case study: Adolescent

Jeremiah is a 15-year-old who was referred for disruptive and combative behaviors at home and at school.

The clinician introduced Jeremiah to the Ladybug tool. Jeremiah told the clinician that there were not enough spots on the ladybug for him to fill out all the issues that were concerning him. This was a great beginning for Jeremiah. He revealed that he was angry with his parents for being so restrictive with him while they allowed his older brother to do whatever he wanted, including smoking marijuana at home. He further revealed that his older brother had physically assaulted his father. Jeremiah was fearful for everyone in the household. He had not told his parents that he had witnessed his brother sniffing other drugs and distributing them from their home.

This was a great beginning conversation for Jeremiah.

IMAGINE A POWERFUL STORM

HANDS-ON

Purpose

To help the child or adolescent determine ways they can feel safe and protected.

What you will need

- ★ Paint
- ★ Paintbrushes
- ★ Colored pencils or a charcoal pencil
- ★ Poster board
- ★ Sounds of a storm

Activity

Talk with the child or adolescent about storms. Play the sound of a storm in the background.

Ask the child or adolescent to paint or draw what a storm looks and feels like.

While they are painting or drawing ask them, what can they do in a storm to feel safe and protected? Is there someone they can go to? Can they turn on the lights or grab a flashlight? Do they need to go to a safe place? Where is their safe place, and who is with them? What else can they do? Can they grab a blanket or a stuffed animal? Can they call a friend?

Finally, ask them if these are the same behaviors that can be used in other situations where they may not feel safe.

Case study: Child

Breanna is a five-year-old who was referred for neglect after being left alone overnight while her mother went out. A neighbor could hear her crying.

The clinician introduced Breanna to the Imagine a Powerful Storm tool. Breanna liked to use the paints. Coincidentally, and unbeknownst to the clinician, Breanna was crying due to fear of the storm the night she had been discovered alone. She revealed that her mom had left her alone on multiple occasions. She revealed she was not afraid of being alone, but she was afraid of storms. When she was alone, she self-comforted by curling up on the couch with her stuffed animal and watching TV. (She had been told not to leave the apartment and she did not have access to a phone.)

This was an excellent tool to get to the heart of what had happened and to begin to identify people who were safe for Breanna.

Case study: Adolescent

Leth is a 14-year-old who was referred after witnessing his friend being struck by random gunfire.

The clinician introduced Leth to the Imagine a Powerful Storm tool. Leth, who is quite artistic, drew a storm with much lightning. Leth revealed that after the shooting incident with his friend it felt like a storm was brewing around him—there was so much activity. His mom, aunt, brothers, and sister were all there for him, and so were his friends. Leth revealed that random shootings had occurred before in his neighborhood, but he had never personally known anyone who had been shot.

This tool identified that Leth had a support system including family and peers, some of whom had also witnessed the trauma.

TUNNEL THINKING

VISUAL/VERBAL

Purpose

To ascertain if the child or adolescent has feelings of hopelessness.

What you will need

★ A cardboard tube, such as from a paper towel

Activity

Talk with the child or adolescent about how our vision is quite wide—we are able to take in many things. We may be looking at each other, but we can also see things in our periphery. Then tell the child or adolescent to look through the cardboard tube. What do they see? Talk about how narrow our vision can become. Explain that sometimes we may be overwhelmed and only feel one strong emotion, such as fear. We may only have one thought, such as the trauma that has happened.

Discuss these issues and ask them if they can see beyond the narrow tunnel of their issue, or their limited thinking or stress-induced thinking and emotions. Discuss ways to look at things from a broader scope, to be able to put things into perspective and to help with their coping.

Ask the child or adolescent, "Are you in a tunnel? Can you see the light ahead, or is it only very dim?"

Case study: Child

Paul is an 11-year-old who was referred for anxiety due to bullying at school.

The clinician introduced Paul to the Tunnel Thinking tool. Paul enjoyed playing with the cardboard tubes, and taped several of them together. He revealed that it was hard for him to think of himself as anything but "trash." Paul was overwhelmed with the other children's and parents' reactions at school to his father's arrest for criminal activities. He had been name-called and threatened by a parent. Paul revealed that he had not shared this with his mother, as she was frequently crying.

This tool was an excellent beginning for Paul to reveal his embarrassment and shame, as well as the need for him to get adult help for the bullying.

Case study: Adolescent

Leth is a 14-year-old who was referred after witnessing his friend being struck by random gunfire.

Leth reluctantly looked through the cardboard tube. He was able to identify that he was having tunnel vision, but so was everyone else in his family and community. He shared that the shooting was all everyone had been talking about for weeks, and much of the discussion he viewed as inappropriate, especially in front of the younger children in the apartment complex he resided in. Leth revealed that his eighth grade graduation was over and there had been no celebration. The clinician and Leth talked about what high school would be like and what he was looking forward to doing during high school.

This tool provided much-needed information as, although Leth had a good support system, many of those individuals had been caught up in the trauma of the shooting event themselves, and were not as available as they once were.

BE GENTLE

HANDS-ON

Purpose

For the child or adolescent to slow down and do something kind, nurturing, and caring for themselves.

What you will need

- ★ An image of a puppy or a kitten

- ★ A soft stuffed puppy or kitten

- ★ Poster board

- ★ Eco glitter

- ★ Bright markers

- ★ Ribbon

- ★ Glue

Activity

Show the child or adolescent the image of the puppy or the kitten. Give them the soft stuffed puppy or kitten to hold.

Ask them to notice how they are currently holding the stuffed animal, or if they could imagine how they would hold a real puppy or kitten. Would they be calm and gentle? Would they talk quietly to the puppy or kitten? They should understand the concept of gentle and kind. Come up with a list of words connected with being gentle and record them on the poster board. Ask the child or adolescent to decorate the poster board with eco glitter and ribbon.

They can take the poster board home and keep it in sight to refer to occasionally.

Read out the following script:

> Do something soft and kind for yourself today, and something soft and kind for someone else tomorrow. Maybe wear a favorite soft sweater or give yourself special permission to go slower and be softer with yourself. One way to be gentle is to check your self-talk and make sure that you are patient and kind with your words to yourself, and then tomorrow make sure that you are patient and kind with your words to others.

Case study: Child

Penelope is an 11-year-old who was referred because her father had been convicted of sexually abusing her younger sisters.

The clinician introduced Penelope to the Be Gentle tool. Penelope started to cry while holding the stuffed animal. She revealed that she had terrible guilt for not helping her younger sisters and for not being a victim herself. Penelope revealed that she had horrible self-talk. Through the tool Penelope was able to create a list of things that she could do to begin to be gentle with herself, including reading for fun, and trying to listen to her music with her ear buds as she used to, instead of listening out for her sisters and being hypervigilant.

This tool helped Penelope to understand that we must also take care of ourselves. It further provided valuable information regarding Penelope's thought process about herself and her sisters.

Case study: Adolescent

Icker is a 15-year-old who was referred for anger and alleged vandalism at his school.

The clinician introduced Icker to the Be Gentle tool. Icker stated that he was taking care of himself and did not let anyone push him around. Icker defined taking care of himself as confronting, in an aggressive manner, peers and others who seemed to conflict with him. Icker and the clinician were able to create a beginning list of how he could take steps to be gentle and calm down. One of the items on his list was taking time to recognize that not everyone was against him. He also liked the idea of taking the time to try a one-minute meditation, which was offered in the session.

This tool helped the clinician and Icker to recognize how overpowering Icker's anger and conflictual behaviors were. It also helped him to recognize that he did not always have to be on the defensive and scanning the environment for issues; rather, he could slow down and turn inwards and take care of himself, even if it was only for a minute.

MORE ALIKE THAN DIFFERENT

HANDS-ON

Purpose

To help the child or adolescent to find strategies for coping. To destigmatize mental health issues by recognizing that many individuals and families experience difficult situations yet, even with the most difficult situations, we still have many commonalities from likes to dislikes, and sometimes we experience similar difficult situations too.

What you will need

- ★ Paper
- ★ Pens or markers

Activity

Explain to the child or adolescent that sometimes, when unexpected and bad things happen to us, we feel quite different from others. What commonalities can they find between themselves and their friends? Do they have the same likes? Do they wear similar clothes? Do they like pizza and pancakes?

What do they perceive as the differences now since the traumatic event happened? Do these differences make it difficult for them to connect with others?

Together, write out a list of their perceived differences since the event and talk through it.

Case study: Child

Violet is a 10-year-old who was referred for anxiety. She has recently been adopted.

The clinician introduced Violet to the More Alike than Different tool. Violet revealed that although she had many similarities to her friends, none of them had been adopted. She said that she was both fearful of how her friends would view her and also ashamed that her mom did not "want" her.

This was a great beginning tool as Violet was able to freely express her fear of rejection and her feelings of abandonment.

Case study: Adolescent

Adonna is a 14-year-old who was referred for issues of anxiety and depression. She has recently been diagnosed with diabetes.

The clinician introduced Adonna to the More Alike than Different tool. Adonna readily stated that she was quite different from her peers. She felt as though she could not participate in many activities because she could not eat the foods that accompanied them. She had recently consumed alcohol and become extremely sick. She did not tell her family, as she was worried about getting into trouble.

This tool was critically important as not only did it help Adonna to express her concerns about fitting in with her peers, but she also shared about her experience of drinking alcohol as someone with diabetes, which can have serious, if not fatal, consequences.

BETTER SELF-CARE

HANDS-ON

Purpose

To identify practical behaviors the child or adolescent can engage in on a regular basis to sustain emotional stability.

What you will need

★ Paper

★ Pens or markers

Activity

Help the child or adolescent identify areas of stress or concern in their current life situation, and explore ways of better self-care. Write them down on paper.

Case study: Child

Nici is an 11-year-old who was referred for stealing food and other objects from school and her group home.

The clinician explained the Better Self-Care tool to Nici. Nici cried and stated that she felt embarrassed about her actions, but that she was not sorry. She revealed that she felt justified in her behaviors as she was not getting her basic needs met. Nici was the youngest member of the group home, by some five years. She was being bullied by some of the other girls, who were stealing food from her as well as basic hygiene products from her toiletry bag. Nici revealed that she had to take the items that she needed from wherever she could, or, on some occasions, she would literally "stink." Nici had taken someone's deodorant and even feminine hygiene products. She also hid food that she took from school in her room in the group home.

Together the clinician and Nici decided that the basic first step in better self-care was to share with the school and with the group home director the issues that Nici was encountering.

Case study: Adolescent

Roger is a 14-year-old who was referred for lack of basic hygiene and combative behaviors, both at school and at home.

The clinician explained the Better Self-Care tool to Roger. Roger stated in a defiant manner that he did not care, and asked why he should care as no one else seemed to care about him. The clinician asked Roger about what had changed for him, as last year he had presented himself in a different manner. Roger revealed much familial discord, including his parents' divorce, his father's affair, and his only sibling leaving for the military. Roger's life had completely changed—he rarely saw his father, and his mother was distraught at not being engaged in Roger's life the way she used to be. Roger was angry and blamed both his mother and father for the upheaval in his life, including the very real possibility that Roger's mother would have to sell the family home, and that he would have to change school districts as he entered high school next year.

The clinician and Roger were able to identify these numerous stressors, and decided to engage Roger's mother in a meaningful and calm conversation about his fears and concerns for the future.

LEARN CALM

Purpose

To enable the child or adolescent to self-soothe and calm themselves.

What you will need

- ★ Poster board

- ★ Calming images, such as sunsets, flowers, bodies of water, etc.

- ★ Different scents, such as lavender, grass, geranium, etc.

- ★ Quiet music or nature sounds

- ★ Paper

- ★ Pens or markers

- ★ Safety scissors

- ★ Glue

Activity

Share with the child or adolescent the intention of helping them to learn to self-soothe. Using the calming images, create a collage of images together that they can refer to that makes them feel calm or soothed. Play quiet music or nature sounds and let them smell the different scents. Ask them to write down how the different scents or the quiet music or nature sounds make them feel.

Case study: Child

Misty is a nine-year-old who was referred for anxiety as a result of issues with adjustment due to loss of sight in one eye.

The clinician introduced Misty to the Learn Calm tool. Misty was able to immediately identify in her life that her new pet support dog and her cat provided her with a sense of wellbeing and comfort. Misty created a collage that was full of animals, pets, and people. She was able to identify while creating her collage that her parents and her older sister had been great supports as she moved through this adjustment to her limited vision.

Case study: Adolescent

Corie is a 15-year-old who was referred for issues of anxiety, which have manifested in irritable bowel syndrome.

The clinician introduced Corie to the Learn Calm tool. Corie revealed that she had a history of anxiety, mostly surrounding school. Her mother, father, and older sister also had a history of anxiety. Corie was familiar with learning to self-soothe. She had participated in meditation and guided visualization with her sister. Corie created a collage of primarily nature images and words. She shared that she remembered her grandfather's cottage, which she visited during many childhood summers with her family. It was a place of quiet. She remembered taking walks and being outside for hours during the summer. She also remembered that she would stargaze with her grandfather and identify the constellations. Corie was happy with her collage and decided to ask her mother to provide her with a copy of a photo of her grandfather's cottage so that she could add it to her collage. She identified that she felt calm and soothed when she thought of the cottage or of nature.

PAUSE

HANDS-ON

Purpose

To help children and adolescents identify internal cues that signal they need to pause before reacting.

What you will need

- ★ Poster board
- ★ Markers or crayons

Activity

Ask the child or adolescent to talk about events when they were able to pause and think about their response before acting. Was it easier to pause in some situations or with some people than others?

Ask the child or adolescent to write out the places and people when it was easier to pause.

Case study: Child

Peter is an 11-year-old who was referred for using markers to deface the bathroom walls at school.

The clinician introduced Peter to the Pause tool. Peter revealed that he had difficulty in pausing in most situations. If he felt anger, he felt like he had to respond immediately. He revealed that that was why he had defaced the bathroom walls. He was able to eventually identify that his mother, grandmother, and math teacher were able to help him to pause. He was able to identify with softer voices and the kindness that these individuals expressed towards him. He created his list and added to it over time.

This was a great beginning tool for Peter to enable him to recognize that he could pause in some situations.

Case study: Adolescent

Keith is a 17-year-old who was referred for fighting behaviors with his siblings.

The clinician introduced Keith to the Pause tool. Keith stated that he could pause most of the time. He was doing well at school, with his parents, and with his friends. He felt as though he was unable to pause with his twin siblings, who seemed to gang up on him or take things from his room or enter his room without permission.

This tool was helpful for Keith as he was able to recognize many times when he was able to pause. He was able to further identify specific interactions that caused real difficulties in terms of lack of control for him.

CLUTTER 1: CLEANING OUT

HANDS-ON

Purpose

To help the child or adolescent "clean out" the extra clutter in their mind.

What you will need

- ★ Poster board or a pizza box with a large outline of a brain taking up most of the surface area

- ★ Thick markers

Activity

Share with the child or adolescent that thoughts and feelings may take up a lot of space in our head and in our day-to-day being, so much so that we may not be able to enjoy or be in the moment.

Ask the child or adolescent to use the prepared outline of the brain to draw thick hash marks of all the thoughts and emotions that are taking up space and cluttering up their emotional and thinking selves. They do not have to label the hash marks with words, as the clinician will be recording the list for them. So they do not have to worry—they can go as fast and freely as they like. Notice how some of the hash marks become very thick and long and some become noticeably short, and when the child or adolescent is pressing extremely hard as they are very emotional about what they are recording.

Attempt to notice a pattern within the thoughts and feelings identified, and determine if there are one or two things that can be done immediately to move in the direction of corrective action.

Remember, this image will also be compared with the image created in the second part of this exercise that follows.

Case study: Child

Luna is an 11-year-old who was referred for suicidal ideation during her parents' divorce.

The clinician introduced Luna to the Clutter 1 tool. Luna created 15 hash marks that represented the familial discord and her own feelings of loss and fear. This was a great opening up for Luna.

Case study: Adolescent

Tyrone is a 17-year-old who was referred for ongoing truancy. He will have to repeat his junior year of high school, unless he is willing to attend Summer School. At this point in time, Tyrone does not want to participate in any school.

The clinician introduced Tyrone to the Clutter 1 tool. Tyrone reacted by saying there was not enough room to place all of the thoughts and emotions he had. Tyrone agreed to add the hash marks, and shared what they represented. By the time he was finished, he felt quite relieved and he exhaled, laughed, and even cried a bit. We counted 47 hash marks, which completely covered and overlapped each other. We noted that most of them represented anger and loss with his family. Tyrone was able to start the difficult story of what was occurring in his life.

CLUTTER 2: CLEAN SLATE

HANDS-ON

Purpose

To help the child or adolescent to move forward from what we found in the previous Clutter 1: Cleaning Out tool, to create a representation of healthier thoughts and emotions, which can lead to goal setting to maintain these thoughts and feelings.

What you will need

* ★ A copy of the work from the Clutter 1: Cleaning Out tool

* ★ A new outline of a brain on the same type of board or box the child or adolescent used for the Clutter 1: Cleaning Out tool: this will be the Clean Slate tool

* ★ Thick markers

Activity

With the child or adolescent, compare the two images of the Clutter 1: Cleaning Out tool and the Clean Slate tool. Discuss what they feel when they review the two. Determine what they may want to place in the Clean Slate tool, if anything. Sometimes simply being aware of how consumed and overloaded they are currently may be enough for them to want to simply experience a new beginning.

Case study: Child

Luna is an 11-year-old who was referred for suicidal ideation during her parents' separation.

The clinician introduced Luna to the Clutter 2: Clean Slate tool. Luna was able to recognize that she was overwhelmed and concentrating on only one area in her life. The clinician validated the current issues that had been consuming her, and then started to help Luna uncover additional thoughts and feelings states that were positive and that she could realistically achieve. Some of these thoughts included spending more time with friends and her best friend, talking to her teacher, and spending time after school in the art room where she could participate in the after-school art club. These activities would provide Luna with hope and excitement, and especially peace and calm, knowing that her best friend and her friends were always there for her to talk to.

Case study: Adolescent

Tyrone is a 17-year-old who was referred for ongoing truancy. He will have to repeat his junior year of high school unless he is willing to attend Summer School. At this point in time, Tyrone does not want to participate in any school.

The clinician introduced Tyrone to the Clutter 2: Clean Slate tool. They compared the previous image from the Clutter 1 tool with the open and blank image of the brain from the Clean Slate tool. Tyrone questioned how it could even be possible to let so much go. The clinician validated Tyrone in his feelings, and recommended that he pursue what could be helpful or make him happy.

Tyrone remembered that before he was labeled a truant he had been on many sports teams, including football and basketball. Tyrone was popular and had many friends throughout that time. He shared that due to his ongoing school issues, at this point he would not be able to return to his sports activities until he was in school and getting appropriate grades. Together, the clinician and Tyrone talked about the idea of reconnecting with friends from school who were supportive and who may be willing to help him catch up with schoolwork. If he considered taking Summer School, there could be a chance of getting back on one of the teams for the sports he loved to do, which, in turn, could lead to opportunities for college. Tyrone placed these items on the list, along with the word "family" and a question mark.

This gave an opportunity for the clinician and Tyrone to explore potential solutions for the discord the family was experiencing.

SUPERHERO

HANDS-ON

Purpose

To help the child and adolescent be creative and ultimately look at needs they may have in terms of power and safety.

What you will need

* ★ A superpower cape or images of Wonder Woman or Superman

* ★ Paper

* ★ Markers

Activity

Ask the child or adolescent, "Can you don a cape and be your own superhero today? How can you power through difficult emotions or feelings? Can you use your superpowers to stay focused or to think positive?"

Case study: Child

Mercy is eight years old and was referred for attention deficit disorder and stress.

The clinician introduced Mercy to the Superhero tool. Mercy said it was easy and that she would like to have the superpower to disappear. She revealed that her peers and some of the teachers continued to get angry with her over what she viewed as her ADHD issues. The clinician challenged Mercy by asking how the disappearing helped. Mercy revealed that not only was it not helpful, but at times the individuals she was engaging with became angry.

Mercy determined that maybe a cape would be helpful because then she may feel more courageous. She identified that being more courageous was the ability to have a conversation about what was really happening with her parents and with her teacher.

Case study: Adolescent

River is a 13-year-old who was referred for sudden issues of withdrawal and social isolation.

The clinician introduced River to the Superhero tool. River stated that there were several superhero powers that he would like, but the most important was the ability to fly. River stated that he wanted to fly away from his school and his mom's house. River noted that after his parents divorced, he had moved with his mom near to his maternal grandmother's home. Both his mom and grandmother inappropriately and repeatedly talked in front of River about his father in a derogatory way. River stated that he was sick and tired of them, and angry, and that he wanted to move back with his dad. The clinician and River decided to have a conversation with his mom to share his distress.

TAKE ACTION

HANDS-ON

Purpose

To identify one issue that is creating fear or anxiety for the child or adolescent.

What you will need

- ★ Poster board or a recycled box

- ★ Markers

Activity

Ask the child or adolescent to describe briefly—very briefly—one issue that is causing fear, anxiety, or distress in some way, and to write this on the poster board or box. Create a list of several things that the child or adolescent could do that would help them to feel better.

Case study: Child

Sophia is a 10-year-old who was referred for anger and for driving her dad's sit-on lawn mower into a lake.

The clinician introduced Sophia to the Take Action tool. Sophia stated that she wished that she could talk to her mom without her mom arguing with her. Sophia and the clinician discussed ways that Sophia could engage her mom. She wanted to invite her mom to their current appointment as her mom was in the waiting room. Before doing so, however, Sophia listed down her most important issue, so that if she became emotional, she could still refer to her list to talk with her mom.

Case study: Adolescent

Tessie is a 14-year-old who is having feelings of overwhelm, anger, and potential violence. He is overwhelmed by feelings of frustration and anger around the way that his friends are treating him—he revealed that he is bisexual.

The clinician and Tessie explored how to slow down, how to center oneself, and to try to come at these things in a different way. Tessie determined that he could talk with his family, and they would advocate for him.

SUNSHINE, RAINBOWS, AND UNICORNS

HANDS-ON

Purpose

For the child or adolescent to learn how to change their emotional state, and to have some fun, silliness, and lightheartedness.

What you will need

- ★ All kinds of stickers, such as unicorns, rainbows, balloons, sunshine, stars, etc.

- ★ Eco glitter

- ★ Paint or paint pens

- ★ Multicolored poster boards

Activity

Share with the child or adolescent that they will be doing some playful, lighthearted activities today. They can have fun with fantasy and create a poster board that reflects fun and whimsy using the various materials provided.

Case study: Child

Toby is a six-year-old who was referred for issues of grief following the death of his live-in maternal grandmother.

The clinician shared with Toby the Sunshine, Rainbows, and Unicorns tool. Toby shared that his grandma used to read a book to him about unicorns, and it was his favorite. He decided to create a poster board that was filled with unicorns and hearts and eco glitter. He had fun creating while he shared with the clinician fun memories from his times with his grandmother.

Case study: Adolescent

Rose is a 16-year-old who was referred for anxiety due to school issues.

The clinician introduced the Sunshine, Rainbows, and Unicorns tool to Rose. She laughed, and revealed that when she was younger, she loved unicorns. She had not thought about fun things in a long time. Her life seemed to be laser-focused on getting the best grades and trying to get into college. As Rose painted and created her poster board, she began to relax and recognize the benefit of fun as a stress reliever, and the importance of having breaks in her studies so that she could be more focused on her work.

SOOTHING COLOR

VISUAL/VERBAL

Purpose

To find a color that helps the child or adolescent to relax or feel calm.

What you will need

★ A color wheel, or printed-out slips of color

Activity

Read out the following script:

> Choose a color that helps you to feel calm, peaceful, or soothed. Give examples from your life. For example, my favorite color is also a color that makes me feel calm and peaceful and it is lavender, light purple.

> Imagine yourself in a room that is entirely that color, and that you are wrapped up snugly in a blanket of that color. Stay with this image for a few minutes. What do you notice in your body? If you are unable to notice anything at first, start with what you are observing, such as noticing calmer breathing, releasing of the shoulders, physical relaxation, etc.

Give the child or adolescent a slip of paper with the color they chose. Ask them to refer to the color and to do this creative visualization process from time to time on their own.

Case study: Child

Dominic is an 11-year-old who was referred for anxiety, panic attacks, and night terrors. Dominic had been molested by his uncle from the age of five to the present day.

The clinician introduced Dominic to the Soothing Color tool. Dominic shared that he had been sleeping in his grandmother's room where she pulled out her "big purple chair" that became a bed, and she covered him in a heavy blanket that was covered in dark purple and flowers. His grandmother's room had a purple light as well as a purple chair, and he felt very safe.

Case study: Adolescent

Kyra is a 15-year-old who was referred for anxiety and panic disorder after an adult male who she sold her undergarments to on the internet sent her a picture of her outside the front of her home. The police were involved in this case.

The clinician introduced Kyra to the Soothing Color tool. Kyra revealed that her favorite color was green for nature; however, lately she felt as though she could not walk alone in nature or in the park, as she was afraid that she would encounter the adult male referred to above. Kyra thought about other shades of green and remembered a time when her family went snorkeling. Kyra talked about the sunlight coming through the surface of the water and the yellow-green colors. She could feel her hair floating and felt safe, even though she was out in the ocean. Kyra was able to identify that she could physically feel herself relax. She agreed to continue to work on her creative visualization to help her with calming and soothing.

FUN WORDS AND IMAGES

HANDS-ON

Purpose

To help the child or adolescent focus on something other than trauma. Using fun words and images can be a much-needed emotional break.

What you will need

- ★ Poster paper
- ★ Glue
- ★ Images of fun things (for younger children)
- ★ Markers
- ★ Safety scissors

Activity

Create a list of fun words, like "zig zag," "tootsie roll," "wiener dog," "sparkle," "giggle," "free," "silly," etc. This is an individual list, words that have a fun meaning for the child or adolescent. Say the words out loud.

For young children who do not have a large vocabulary, find and cut out fun images and stick them on paper. See how emotions change as we focus on different words and images.

Case study: Child

Hazel is six years old. She was referred for sadness and difficulty transitioning between her parents' homes after their divorce.

The clinician explained the Fun Words and Images tool. Hazel shared that she had fun with dogs, kittens, paint, and games. Many of her fun words and images she only experienced in one house now. It appeared that one parent had all the animals and games. So, when she spent time at the other parent's, she felt lonely and uncomfortable. She did remember, however, that she was painting and learning weaving at that parent's home.

Case study: Adolescent

Arnold is a 14-year-old who was referred for adjustment issues in his new school. He is having difficulty making friends and failing several classes.

The clinician introduced Arnold to the Fun Words and Images tool. Arnold shared that he had not had fun since he moved. He used to laugh freely and play with his friend's two dogs and run around the neighborhood. He even had a potbelly pig as a neighbor. Now it was difficult for him to relate to anyone. His classmates were quite different. He still liked dogs, potbelly pigs, baseball, etc.

The clinician and Arnold agreed to make a more comprehensive list of fun words and images and to try to find one person in his class who had a similar interest.

Part 2

POSITIVE THINKING

WHAT CAN YOU TRANSPLANT?

VISUAL/VERBAL

Purpose

To remember what good things the child or adolescent is already doing that they would like to bring forward or carry forward to help them cope or feel better.

What you will need

★ An image of a person moving or transplanting flowers or plants from one area to another

Activity

Show the child or adolescent the image of the person transplanting flowers or plants from one area to another. Discuss what "transplanting" means. Use this as a metaphor for what they would like to carry with them or transplant into their life now.

Case study: Child

Lucia is a five-year-old kindergartener. She was referred for grief and displacement after her mother died.

The clinician explained the What Can You Transplant? tool to Lucia. Lucia immediately responded and identified that she took the cat with her everywhere—Lucia carried a small stuffed cat with her. This cat was later identified as a transition object that Lucia had used for several years when going from her mother's home to her grandmother's home for care. She liked to hold onto it and squeeze her face into it when she was sad or scared. The stuffed animal smelled like her mom and her home, and it provided her with comfort.

Case study: Adolescent

Zina is a 15-year-old student who was referred for unwillingness to meet with her father during weekly visitation.

The clinician introduced Zina to the What Can You Transplant? tool. Zina replied that there was not a lot she could transplant into her dad's home. She felt as though when she tried to talk with her dad, he ignored her or was not interested in what she had to say. The clinician and Zina discussed the idea that in the past her dad was interested in her artwork and papers that she wrote. Together they talked about how Zina could bring her new artwork or papers to share with her dad.

SPIRALING

VISUAL/VERBAL

Purpose

To help the child or adolescent determine if they are stuck in a negative spiral of thoughts or behaviors.

What you will need

★ A drawing or photograph of a spiral, the size of a standard sheet of paper or larger

Activity

Show the child or adolescent the drawing or photograph of the spiral. Talk about the idea of spiraling, of going around and around on a set of thoughts or behaviors without a solution. Notice that many of these thoughts and behaviors originate in the middle, in the center of the spiral.

Case study: Child

Connor is an eight-year-old who was referred for ongoing issues of fighting behaviors in the classroom and at home.

The clinician introduced Connor to the Spiraling tool. Connor identified that the center in his spiral was anger. He stated that he was not sure where the anger came from. He stated that the anger just came on, and when it started, he could not stop it until he had acted out and become exhausted.

Case study: Adolescent

Genesis is a 13-year-old who was referred for ongoing issues of verbal attacks on authority figures, including her teachers, parents, and the school principal.

The clinician explained the Spiraling tool to Genesis. Genesis was able to identify that the center of the spiral was her being triggered by a perceived criticism. When she was triggered, she let out a barrage of insults at the person she perceived to be attacking her. This had led to her being suspended and ultimately placed in two new schools within a one-year period.

This was a great opening up for Genesis.

TICKLE, LAUGHTER

VISUAL/VERBAL

Purpose

To help the child or adolescent remember that they have experienced good, fun times even though right now may be exceedingly difficult for them. To help the child or adolescent remember a time when they genuinely laughed.

What you will need

★ Images of people laughing

Activity

Share with the child or adolescent the images of people laughing. Notice facial features, if people are holding their bellies when they laugh, whether tears are streaming out of their eyes when they laugh, if they are covering their mouths when they laugh. What differences do they notice? Ask them to recall when they had a genuine, deep belly laugh. What did they do? Did they cover their mouth, hold their belly, etc.?

Case study: Child

Benjamin is a seven-year-old who was referred after his parents divorced.

Benjamin has a placement with both parents, although he frequently shared that he was having trouble having fun or feeling joy. The clinician introduced the Tickle, Laughter tool to Benjamin. Benjamin stated that his dad used to tickle him often, and sometimes his parents would end up rolling on the floor and tickling each other. He remembered many happy times with his family.

He revealed that his family no longer "has fun." Together, Benjamin and the clinician were able to "find" times when Benjamin had had fun recently and with his parents individually. They talked about how he did still have fun and laughter.

Case study: Adolescent

Lucas is a 13-year-old who was referred for issues of social difficulty with his peers.

The clinician introduced Lucas to the Tickle, Laughter tool. Lucas revealed that it seemed as though over the past year he had not been able to be as open with his friends, and that they seemed to be much more judgmental. He revealed that things that used to be funny no longer seemed to be.

CHANGING LANES

VISUAL/VERBAL

Purpose

To help the child or adolescent notice when they are repeating old, unhealthy behaviors, and to attempt to do something that will be more helpful or healthier.

What you will need

★ An image of a car or bicycle approaching a bump or pothole in the road that will require the car or bicycle to change lanes

Activity

Have the child or adolescent look at the image of the car or bicycle needing to change lanes. Use this image as a metaphor to identify what they may see as a potential difficulty in their healing process.

Case study: Child

Nova is a 10-year-old who was referred for issues with transition between households.

The clinician introduced Nova to the Changing Lanes tool. Nova discussed that her parents did not allow her to bring toys or clothing from one household to the other. It was discovered that even though Nova had been transitioning for over six months, she was still struggling. Nova identified a favorite stuffed animal at one home and a favorite pillow at the other. She wanted to take these two objects back and forth, to both households.

This gave important information for the clinician—the need to discuss the importance of a transition object as a coping tool for Nova.

Case study: Adolescent

Simone is a 17-year-old who was referred for issues of anxiety and the threat of self-harm.

The clinician introduced Simone to the Changing Lanes tool. Simone discussed that she could see a huge pothole in the road that seemed to take up the entire lane. She identified this pothole as her fear of college and not being able to pay for college. Simone was waiting to see where she was admitted and what kind of aid she would receive. She revealed that during the last six months she had been anxious and had started to bite the inside of her mouth and had been biting her fingernails to the quick. She also revealed that she had started to use over-the-counter medication to help her sleep.

POSITIVE SELF

Purpose

To help the child or adolescent remember or discover a positive attribute that they can use for coping.

What you will need

- ★ Paper

- ★ Markers or gel pens

Activity

Together write a list of positive attributes with the child or adoles-cent. Remember that the list is of positive attributes in general, not necessarily specific to the child or adolescent. Ask them to circle some of the attributes that they possess. As they are working, they may discover new attributes in themselves that they can add to the list.

Case study: Child

Paisley is a 10-year-old who was referred for issues of aggression at school and at home.

The clinician introduced the Positive Self tool to Paisley. Together they proceeded to create a list of positive attributes. Paisley revealed that she had had a lot of difficulty feeling good about herself, ever since her half-sister moved into the home. The clinician and Paisley determined that one of Paisley's attributes was her ability to communicate. Paisley decided that she would talk with her mom about her feelings about her half-sister.

121

Case study: Adolescent

Charles is a 14-year-old who was referred for issues of tardiness in school and failing several classes as a freshman.

The clinician introduced the Positive Self tool to Charles. Charles was able to create a list of positive attributes. He was able to identify several positive personal attributes. He revealed through this list that now that he was in high school, his attributes were not as distinguished as they had been in middle school. This was helpful information as Charles was readily able to identify that he was judging himself against his peers. He further revealed that he had been the number one ranked student all through middle school. Now that he was in high school, he was meeting peers who were challenging, and this was new for him.

STRONG ROOTS

VISUAL/VERBAL

Purpose

To remind the child or adolescent that they are strong, resilient, and flexible, even during times when they may be uprooted.

What you will need

- ★ An image of a tree with roots

- ★ An image of a tree in a storm, bending

- ★ An image of a tree after a storm—missing leaves or a branch, but still intact

Activity

Show the image of the tree with roots to the child or adolescent. Discuss its deep roots and how it keeps growing and stretching up to the sky. Show the second image of the tree in a storm bending, but still having firm roots. Show the third image of the tree after the storm. It may be missing leaves or a branch, but it still has its roots, and it is still growing.

Case study: Child

Bella is 11 years old and was referred for adjustment issues after being reunified with her mother after a one-year separation.

The clinician introduced Bella to the Strong Roots tool. Bella shared that her family had been through many things, but throughout the time when their mom was away she could rely on her grandmother and her older sister. She referred to both her grandmother and her older sister as being strong. She was now concerned that her mother was angry at her grandmother, and that she would not be able to see her grandmother as much. She revealed that even though she missed her grandmother, her older sister was always there for her and "always strong." Bella wanted to be as strong as her sister and her grandmother.

Case study: Adolescent

Max is a 17-year-old who was referred for planning on transitioning to independent living on his 18th birthday.

The clinician introduced Max to the Strong Roots tool. Max stated that he could relate to all the images of the trees. He revealed that he had been through many difficulties with his family not being available. He had been in foster care or group home care since he was 12. He now recognized that he was aging out of the system. However, he felt quite strong. He was graduating from high school and going to college with a friend he had met in high school. They planned to open their own company at some point, in electrics or plumbing. Max felt like he had weathered many storms, but he was also extraordinarily strong and deeply rooted in himself.

This was quite a memorable session with Max.

PERSONAL POWER

VISUAL/VERBAL

Purpose

To discover a personal power or strength that the child or adolescent can identify and use that has been successful in the past.

What you will need

★ Only you

Activity

Discuss the idea of inner resources and how these can be tapped into. Most of us have many inner resources, but during difficult times, we may forget what has worked for us in the past.

Ask the child or adolescent to identify a resource, power, or strength that they have not used in a while. Can friends or family see this resource? What do they need to do to gain momentum to use it again to bring about their own internal change?

Case study: Child

Madelyn is a seven-year-old who was referred for night terrors and sleepwalking.

The clinician introduced Madelyn to the Personal Power tool. Madelyn was a little embarrassed and shy, and revealed to the clinician that in the past she did not have a personal power and reverted to thumb sucking or chewing the inside of her mouth. Madelyn and the clinician talked more and found that in the past Madelyn would reach out to her older sister, who was currently away at college. Madelyn also discovered that in the past she had the power to use her self-talk to calm after waking up from a nightmare.

Case study: Adolescent

Damian is a 15-year-old who was referred for issues of depression.

The clinician introduced Damian to the Personal Power tool. Damian was able to identify several inner resources and strengths that he had and had used to help him with his depression. Damian identified that he frequently used checking his self-talk in the past. He would identify his self-talk and change it when it was negative or destructive. He also identified that he had used exercise in the past to jump-start feeling better. He realized that exercise was one area that he could start on immediately to help improve his mood. He could also restart his self-talk journaling practice.

REAL HAPPINESS

VISUAL/VERBAL

Purpose

To help the child or adolescent to recognize all-or-none or black-and-white thinking. To help them remember that they have experienced genuinely happy times in their lives. And to help them expand out of a narrow box of thinking to move towards hope.

What you will need

★ Only you

Activity

Ask the child or adolescent to think about a time when they were genuinely happy, to think about it clearly with all their senses. Were they at peace? Did they feel overall wellbeing? Ask them to notice if, after remembering the time, they notice any changes in their body or feelings state.

Case study: Child

Tenisha is a nine-year-old who was referred for feelings of anger and rage that caused her to damage property at school. She had moved to live with her aunt.

The clinician explained the Real Happiness tool to Tenisha. Initially, she responded that she had never been happy, and challenged the clinician as to why she would even want to be happy. The clinician explained that sometimes our feelings are so big that they consume our ability to think about other emotions. Tenisha finally revealed that even though she had been successfully placed with her aunt, she was full of rage towards her mother and her eldest sister, who had been accused of selling drugs from their home. Tenisha shared two memories that were helpful. One was with her four siblings, her aunt, and her mom together, celebrating a birthday. Another was from Christmas, when she enjoyed the anticipation of the Christmas dinner and festivities.

Case study: Adolescent

Kendor is a 14-year-old who was referred for issues of depression and alcohol use. He was living with his uncle while his dad was away on active service.

The clinician explained the Real Happiness tool to Kendor. Kendor stated that there had been a lot of trouble in his life recently, and not that much happiness. He could recall multiple times in the past when he had genuine happiness, particularly when his dad was home—Kendor's dad was in the military. His mother and sister were now living with his maternal aunt until his dad returned. Kendor was not sure when his dad would be returning home. In addition, he revealed that his uncle frequently drank alcohol, and Kendor had been stealing it.

Kendor can remember many happy times with his entire family until his dad left. Now, he stated, "Nothing is the same." Kendor revealed one of his favorite things was pizza and movie night, which his mother had "made sure" occurred weekly. The clinician and Kendor explored the idea of creating another pizza and movie night with his mom and sister and extended family. Kendor also recognized that drinking alcohol to unwind was not healthy, and he was able to identify that his uncle seemed to drink a lot and not notice when Kendor took alcohol from him.

DEPICT YOURSELF AND YOUR STRENGTHS

HANDS-ON

Purpose

For the child or adolescent to remember their strengths, power, and unique abilities, and to foster self-esteem and self-efficacy.

What you will need

★ Large poster board, sheet of paper, or cardboard

★ Paint

★ Paintbrushes

★ Markers or crayons

Activity

Get big—using a large poster board, sheet of paper, or cardboard, ask the child or adolescent to write down, or draw or paint images that show how they are strong, creative, and wise.

Case study: Child

D'Angelo is a seven-year-old who was referred for issues of neglect. He is currently living in kinship with his aunt. He has supervised visitations with his biological mother, from whom he was removed.

The clinician explained the Depict Yourself and Your Strengths tool and D'Angelo started to create an exceedingly small drawing. The clinician encouraged him to get bigger. D'Angelo laughed and drew a large drawing of himself walking his aunt's dog. He shared that when he walked the dog, he felt extraordinarily strong and free. He could run and play with the dog, and he had created several new toys for the dog. He was also teaching the dog new behaviors.

D'Angelo was able to feel and name strength, freedom, and creativity in what he did on a day-to-day basis.

Case study: Adolescent

Moncha is a 14-year-old who was referred for depression. Moncha's family has a history of depression, on both his mother's and his father's side.

The clinician explained the Depict Yourself and Your Strengths tool to Moncha. Moncha drew a large drawing of himself surrounded by many people, music, books, trees, and animals. He stated that he had episodic depression and that he found great strength in talking with his family and his best friend, who also suffered from depression. He revealed that he knew when a new episode of depression was beginning and he tried to use music, books, and his family's dogs to help him cope. Moncha understood that he had many strengths, and that he felt better in nature. Finally, he had recently shared with his family that he wanted to learn the guitar, a new learning experience for him, as he had never been motivated to try an instrument before.

SCRAPBOOK OF THE HEART

Purpose

For the child or adolescent to be able to identify happy memories as a means of comfort.

What you will need

- ★ Red construction paper
- ★ Safety scissors
- ★ Sticky notes
- ★ Markers or colored pens

Activity

Ask the child or adolescent to cut out a large heart from the construction paper. Thinking about special memories they would like to keep, ask them to write these out onto sticky notes, and to place these on the paper heart. The child or adolescent can keep some of the sticky notes to encourage them to think of more special memories.

Case study: Child

Piaga is an eight-year-old who was referred for issues of grief and depression following her parents' divorce.

Piaga enjoyed cutting out the heart. She was able to identify several memories that featured her family pre-divorce. The clinician asked Piaga if she had any more recent memories that she would like to add with her mom and dad, individually. Piaga was able to identify several memories of each parent individually that were warm and loving. These memories comforted her and gave her hope for future good memories.

Case study: Adolescent

Princess is a 17-year-old who was referred for physical violence at school and at home. She has numerous charges pending.

The clinician introduced Princess to the Scrapbook for the Heart tool. Princess was frustrated and angry. She stated that her memories were all bad, both at home and at school. On further encouragement, Princess found one memory that she was holding onto, and it was one word—"Mama"—which is how she referred to her maternal grandmother.

This was a great beginning as Princess was able to identify someone in her life who was "good" to her. This allowed the clinician and Princess a starting place of positivity versus exclusively anger.

SOW YOUR OWN HAPPINESS

HANDS-ON

Purpose

To remind the child or adolescent that sometimes when they have anger or hurt it is easy and may feel comforting to think about the other person's demise, or to hope that pain befalls them.

What you will need

★ Paper

★ Gel pens or markers

Activity

Acknowledge the child's or adolescent's pain and their story about the person who caused the pain. Discuss that the idea of waiting or looking for that person to have pain is not helping them to get out of pain right now. What is something that they could do right now to move towards happiness? Create a list together and write it down. Ask the child or adolescent what they can do to create happiness for themselves now.

Case study: Child

Nini is a 10-year-old who was referred after suffering physical abuse by her biological father.

Nini presented with a chipped tooth and a fractured arm. The clinician introduced Nini to the Sow Your Own Happiness tool. Nini revealed that she felt much safer now that her dad had been incarcerated. The abuse that she had suffered occurred on several occasions, but was never reported. Nini revealed that she was angry at her dad for hurting her, and at times for hurting her mom and her brother. She did not want her dad to ever be released from prison, and she and her brother secretly talked about him being beaten up. Nini recognized that these types of conversations with her brother also made her feel sick to her stomach. She was tired and sad and anxious. She revealed that when her cast came off, she wanted to go to the community pool. Right now, though, she could go to her best friend's house and dangle her feet in the water of their back yard pool and talk with her. She could also watch movies and eat pizza with her mom and brother. When the pain became less intense, she could sleep over at her grandparents, which was fun and comforting.

Together the clinician and Nini created a list that Nini starred, and they highlighted the activities in the order that Nini thought would work.

Case study: Adolescent

Levi is a 16-year-old who was referred for viewing domestic violence committed by his father on his mother.

The clinician introduced Levi to the Sow Your Own Happiness tool. Levi revealed that after witnessing his father hurting his mother, he hoped that his father would be in prison for an exceedingly long time. Levi revealed that one of the immediate actions he could take to gain a feeling of wellbeing would be to drive his mother to her physical therapy appointments; now that he had his temporary license, he was able to help her. He also wanted to be able to hang out with his friends more, but was concerned about his mother being alone. He reasoned that if his grandmother or his aunt could stay with his mother, he could leave the house and just have a break and be with his friends.

Together, the clinician and Levi created a list of fun activities that Levi could participate in if someone were helping his mother. This was a great beginning for Levi.

RACING STRIPES

Purpose

To help the child or adolescent identify their strengths.

What you will need

- ★ Images of cars with racing stripes (that can be written on)

- ★ Pen

Activity

Share with the child or adolescent the images of the racing cars. Ask them to think about the stripes as representing their strengths.

Ask them to identify three strengths within themselves and to write them on the racing stripes. They can take their images home to help them remember their strengths.

Case study: Child

Nico is a nine-year-old who was referred for anxiety and depression after her biological mother was incarcerated.

The clinician introduced Nico to the Racing Stripes tool. Nico was able to identify that she was doing well in school, that she loved her grandparents, her sibling, and her dad, and that they loved her—she felt safe now.

This was a good beginning to opening up for Nico.

Case study: Adolescent

Pearl is a 15-year-old who was referred for hiding food in her room and for morbid obesity.

The clinician introduced Pearl to the Racing Stripes tool. Pearl revealed that even though she was embarrassed that she had been caught hiding food again in her room, it required her to pay attention and be accountable for her health. On the racing car stripes Pearl wrote "personal accountability," "beginning exercise," and "willingness to meet with a physician to talk about weight loss goals and a plan." She stated that she did not want to get diabetes like her cousin due to being overweight.

SORTING OUT

VISUAL/VERBAL

Purpose

To help identify individuals who are resources for the child or adolescent, and who are readily available in their life during times of stress and confusion.

What you will need

★ A photo of a 100-piece and a 1000-piece jigsaw puzzle

Activity

Show the child or adolescent both photos and ask them to imagine how daunting a puzzle can be with 1000 pieces compared with 100. Ask them to identify individuals in their life to whom they could go to seek help in sorting things out such as the 1000 puzzle pieces or confusion in their life.

Show the child or adolescent that sometimes we need to ask for help from others to help us sort out feelings. Who are their resources to help them sort things out?

Case study: Child

Winn is an 11-year-old who was referred due to confusion and anxiety towards her mother's long-term hospitalization.

The clinician introduced Winn to the Sorting Out tool. Winn shared that she did not know what was happening to her mom physically, and was worried that she was in pain and perhaps would not make it home. Winn further shared that she was embarrassed to ask questions because everyone was treating her like a small child.

This tool allowed Winn to communicate strong feelings about her mother's health state.

Case study: Adolescent

Adrian is a 15-year-old who was referred for issues of acting out in school including name-calling, bullying, and incivility.

The clinician explained the Sorting Out tool to Adrian. Adrian did not want to participate initially, and then stated that he had been having issues with several older teens who were bullying him into illegal activities.

This tool allowed the clinician to move forward in helping Adrian to identify these troublesome issues.

PAINT THE DARKNESS, PAINT THE LIGHT, FEEL THE DIFFERENCE

HANDS-ON

Purpose

The purpose of this activity is to help the child or adolescent to remember that we can change our feelings states, and move from darkness into light.

What you will need

- ★ Paint
- ★ Paintbrushes
- ★ Poster board

Activity

Ask the child or adolescent to paint their representation of darkness and then their representation of light. Ask them to notice differences in their feelings states as they engage in each activity.

Case study: Child

Morse is a 11-year-old who was referred for issues of sadness, isolation, and withdrawal. His family had recently relocated, his twin brothers had moved out of the home, and his dog had passed away.

The clinician introduced Morse to the Paint the Darkness, Paint the Light, Feel the Difference tool. Morse reluctantly used black, blue, and streaks of white paint to demonstrate the darkness. He then painted lightness with light blue and white paint. Morse shared with the clinician that when he concentrated, he could feel the difference in his body between light and dark, but lately he just felt darkness. He further revealed he no longer looked forward to school and was having difficulty making new friends. He was missing his old friends, his old house, and his dog.

This tool allowed Morse to discuss the complex stressors that he was currently facing.

Case study: Adolescent

Elora is a 16-year-old who was referred for issues of anger and resentment towards her parents for relocating to a different State during her junior year of high school.

The clinician introduced Elora to the Paint the Darkness, Paint the Light, Feel the Difference tool. Elora painted her mother's and father's names on the poster board before covering them with red and black paint. She then painted her poster board white on white. Elora revealed that she was more angry at her parents than she was sad. She stated that everyone was saying that she was depressed, but she felt so angry that she could not speak. And she did not feel as though her parents would listen if she tried. Elora further revealed that her white-on-white painting represented feeling numb or disassociated at times, although she was, at times, able to enjoy texting her old friends and feeling lightness.

This tool was a powerful way for Elora to express her many feelings.

FREEZE OR ZAP UNWANTED THOUGHTS

HANDS-ON

Purpose

To learn to control unwanted thoughts.

What you will need

- ★ Construction paper
- ★ Safety scissors
- ★ Tape
- ★ Glue
- ★ 3-D cardboard shapes

Activity

Share with the child or adolescent that they are going to create an imaginary device that will allow them to freeze or zap unwanted thoughts.

Sometimes our mind keeps coming back to the same thoughts. It is important to learn to control those thoughts. The child or adolescent can create any representation they want—maybe a laser gun or an ice wand, or wherever their creative mind takes them.

Read out the following script:

We are doing this to stop the bad thoughts. When we are remembering something, our brain does not know the difference between remembering and being there. If we are remembering sad or scary thoughts or images, we will feel fear, and our body will respond as if we were there. We might feel tension or tightness in our body, or we might feel nauseous, like throwing up. When those thoughts come in, we can freeze or zap them. We can imagine them breaking up and disappearing.

Case study: Child

Libby is a six-year-old who was referred for witnessing domestic violence. Her father is currently incarcerated.

The clinician introduced Libby to the Freeze or Zap Unwanted Thoughts tool. Libby created a wand with a large white feather at the tip. She revealed that she kept having images of the domestic violence by her father against her mother. She stated that she was fearful that he would come back and hurt or kill her mother. Libby had witnessed numerous occurrences of this nature between her father and mother. Libby agreed that every time she had the thought, she would pick up her wand and bring it to her mother. Libby's mother agreed to comfort Libby, and to let her know she was safe.

This tool was a great way for Libby to control her thoughts and to be able to have comfort from her mother, whom she was overly concerned about.

Case study: Adolescent

Nixon is a 15-year-old who was referred for anxiety.

The clinician introduced Nixon to the Freeze or Zap Unwanted Thoughts tool. Nixon shared that he had so many unwanted thoughts that he didn't know where to start. While Nixon worked with a 3-D triangle, he talked about moving from homelessness into a shelter. He revealed that he was fearful in the shelter and kept having thoughts of someone hurting his younger brother or sister. He further revealed that some nights he did not close his eyes until it was lights out.

This tool allowed for Nixon to share his overwhelming fear for the safety of his family.

FUN, BRIEF MOMENTS OF JOY

HANDS-ON

Purpose

For the child or adolescent to remember feelings of joy and to recreate an activity that had been fun or joyful in the past.

What you will need

- ★ Images of children or adolescents engaging in fun behaviors, such as swimming, reading, riding bikes, playing games, etc.

- ★ Paper

- ★ Pens or markers

Activity

Show the child or adolescent the age-appropriate images of having fun. Ask them what is something fun that they have done in the past that they really enjoyed. Create a list together. Then ask which item on the list could be chosen to do today.

Case study: Child

Leisa is a seven-year-old who was referred after moving in with her family to her maternal grandmother's house, due to her grandmother's need for care.

The clinician introduced Leisa to the Fun, Brief Moments of Joy tool. Leisa revealed that since the move to her grandmother's house there had not been much time for fun. Her family used to play games, go on trips, and spend time watching movies and making pizza. Leisa revealed that time was now spent talking about her grandmother, or watching her parents taking care of her grandmother. She further revealed that her parents were so consumed that they hadn't been able to do a fun family activity in a long time.

This tool helped the clinician to understand the complexity of this multigenerational household and the needs of the family.

Case study: Adolescent

Jerald is a 17-year-old who was referred for issues of anxiety with panic disorder.

The clinician introduced Jerald to the Fun, Brief Moments of Joy tool. Jerald revealed that as recently as a few months ago he had participated in many things that were fun and that gave him a sense of joy. He shared that he played guitar and basketball, and enjoyed watching his brother in professional bicycle races. He further revealed that he no longer participated in any fun activities because he was consumed with high school and getting into a good college.

This tool helped the clinician to recognize the tremendous stressors that Jerald was encountering in his quest to be admitted into college.

HOPE AND LOOKING FORWARD

Purpose

For the child or adolescent to create, foster, and protect a sense of hope for the future, a sense of a time when things will be different or better.

What you will need

- ★ Images of rainbows, sunshine, happy children, or adolescents engaging in life through conversation or play, families engaging together, etc.

- ★ Magazines

- ★ Poster board

- ★ Safety scissors

- ★ Glue

- ★ Pens or markers

- ★ Stickers that represent hope and happiness, such as hearts, sunshine, four-leaf clovers, rainbows, stars, etc.

Activity

Talk with the child or adolescent about the word "hope" and what it means to them. Help them to identify feelings of expectation about specific good things that they would like to happen in their lives. The hopes that are identified may be short-term or longer-term desires. Ask them to write these down and stick them on the poster board.

Case study: Child

Rodell is a 10-year-old who was referred for help with transitioning back to her home from foster care.

The clinician explained to Rodell the Hope and Looking Forward tool. Rodell placed stickers of stars, sunshine, hearts, and rainbows on the top and sides of her poster board. As she worked on this, she shared that her biggest hope was that her mom could stay healthy and off alcohol. Together the clinician and Rodell recorded and numbered Rodell's hopes such as sleepovers with friends back at her home, eating her mom's brownies, doing homework with her mom, and generally spending time with her mom. While Rodell listed her hopes, she also cut out images from magazines of kids playing and a mom and child reading together. She glued these images and others onto her poster board.

Case study: Adolescent

Wilson is a 17-year-old who was referred for failing his senior year of high school due to truancy and not turning in assignments.

The clinician explained the Hope and Looking Forward tool to Wilson. Wilson appeared agitated. He stated that "sure," he would love any of the images, but these would never be his reality. Wilson revealed that his family did not have much "hope" for him. He had engaged in several behaviors this year that were destructive. In addition, he could not see being successful in technical college because of his learning difficulties. Wilson did not have an Individualized Education Plan (IEP).

Through the discussion Wilson was able to share that he wanted to study to become an electrician or a plumber. He further revealed that he could do his practical education with his uncle, who was a licensed plumber. Wilson talked about the plumbing profession as one that was stable and well paid, and one where he could interact with people on a regular basis rather than sitting in front of a computer at a desk all day.

Starting with the plumbing career, Wilson was able to list several hopes including owning a home or renting an apartment, helping his own family monetarily, and having a family of his own.

DRIP, DROP, DROP

HANDS-ON

Purpose

To introduce the child or adolescent to the concept of patterns, including visual and auditory patterns. Patterns help individuals to cope and to also notice behaviors that may be helpful or harmful.

What you will need

- ★ Watercolor paint
- ★ Different-sized paintbrushes
- ★ Water (for rinsing paintbrushes)
- ★ Poster board or recycled cardboard

Activity

Explain to the child or adolescent that they will be choosing watercolor paint to mix up and then create large drops of paint, dripping onto their poster board or cardboard. As they allow the watercolor paint to drip off the paintbrush they may notice the sound of the paint splattering or the drops looking similar or different. Ask them to remain incredibly quiet and to begin to listen to the sound of the paint dropping onto the board, noticing the patterns that the paint creates.

Case study: Child

Eliza is an eight-year-old who was referred for issues of anxiety and difficulty going back to school after summer vacation. She lives with her father during the summer and her mother during the school year.

The clinician introduced Eliza to the Drip, Drop, Drop tool. Eliza chose a large white pizza box. She allowed the colored water to drop onto the board; she chose the same color repeatedly—dark blue. She eventually changed her color to completely pink. Eliza and the clinician could hear and see the patterns from the water-color drops; they allowed her to focus and relax, and for a short period of time to be calm and peaceful, and to have a break from ongoing familial issues.

Case study: Adolescent

Samantha is a 16-year-old who was referred for severe anxiety with panic attacks, depression, and self-harm. Her mother had recently relapsed for the third time this year from alcohol addiction.

The clinician introduced Samantha to the Drip, Drop, Drop tool. Samantha shared that some of the only times that she could be calm was when she was crafting. Samantha chose a recycled pizza box. She started to drop the watercolor paint onto it, and then asked if it would be okay to splatter it a couple of times. She splattered the paint, and it was even louder. She repeatedly splattered the paint until there was no longer room on the card-board. She asked for another piece of cardboard and resumed the drip process. She chose yellow and green as her watercolors. Samantha shared that after splattering the paint she was able to rid herself of some of the nervous energy that she had. She shared that the feeling of being patient and having the paint slowly drop off the thick paintbrush was calming. She asked to take her paint-ing home and said she would do this again to help her calm down and feel peace.

WHAT NEXT?

HANDS-ON

Purpose

To allow the child or adolescent to determine what would be the next step that they could legitimately take and be successful at.

What you will need

★ Paper

★ Markers

★ Eco glitter

★ Star stickers

Activity

Introduce the child or adolescent to the idea that they will be creating a list of one or two positive, happy activities that they could have success participating in.

Case study: Child

Luna is an 11-year-old who was referred for suicidal ideation during her parents' separation.

Luna was able to build on previous tools. The clinician introduced Luna to the What Next? tool. She created a list that stemmed from her close relationships with her peers and her best friend. Luna's best friend's mom was also Luna's teacher. She was aware of what was occurring for Luna, and was incredibly open to helping her. She had had Luna over for dinner and sleepovers while the distress within the family was being sorted out.

Luna created a list of several fun activities that would give her not only a sense of accomplishment but also a sense of showing appreciation for her friends and her friend's mom. Luna decided she would like to make a card and treats for her friend's mom and her friends. Luna stated that she was feeling better and that it made her feel extra-special to give something to someone else, as her best friend's mom had become someone Luna could rely on and talk to. She finished her chart by adding eco glitter and star stickers.

Case study: Adolescent

Tyrone is a 17-year-old who was referred for ongoing truancy. He will have to repeat his junior year of high school unless he is willing to attend Summer School. At this point in time, Tyrone does not want to participate in any school.

The clinician introduced Tyrone to the What Next? tool. Building on his use of some of the other activities, Tyrone was able to identify several action steps that he could take. He noted that if it worked out with his new tutor, he planned to attend Summer School so that he could resume his personal life with his friends from school. He also listed wanting to participate in football camp during the summer, if he was allowed to by the school. He shared that he was feeling on track; however, he wanted to confront his family at some point over his intense feelings surrounding family life.

BE SOLUTION-FOCUSED

HANDS-ON

Purpose

For the child or adolescent to stay focused on possible solutions rather than on the problem.

What you will need

- ★ Paper
- ★ Pens or markers

Activity

Introduce the child or adolescent to the concept of being solution-focused. Explain that sometimes we are so focused on the problem that we can forget there may be a solution. Create a list of possible solutions and write these up.

Case study: Child

Teena is a 10-year-old who was referred for pulling her sister's hair and then punching her in the mouth—her sister lost a baby tooth in the altercation.

The clinician introduced Teena to the Be Solution-Focused tool. Teena revealed that there was no talking to her sister—she simply took Teena's things and ruined them. The clinician focused on behaviors that Teena could do to protect her things rather than acting out on her sister after something had been destroyed. Teena and the clinician created a list of several solution-focused behaviors, including telling the babysitter what was occurring, removing items out of her sister's reach, and determining which toys Teena would allow her sister to play with, and have time to play together. Teena agreed to give these ideas a try.

Case study: Adolescent

Tencil is a 14-year-old who was referred for low self-esteem and issues of school attendance.

The clinician introduced Tencil to the Be Solution-Focused tool. Tencil shared that it was hard for him to attend school because people called him names and made fun of his family. His father had recently been incarcerated for armed robbery, which involved youth in the community. Tencil was able to discern one solution that would help, which was having the school administration be aware of the name-calling and potential bullying that was occurring. The clinician and Tencil also talked about the idea that he and his father were separate people, and that up until recently things had been going well for Tencil in school.

OLD THINGS

VISUAL/VERBAL

Purpose

To have the child or adolescent remove objects that are painful and replace them with happy memories or inspirational messages.

What you will need

★ Only you

Activity

Ask the child or adolescent to think about their bedroom. Ask them about objects that are uncomfortable or that bring up bad or sad memories. Ask them to identify objects that remind them of happy times or that make them feel happy or comforted. Once the painful objects are identified, ask if they could be boxed or donated or simply moved out of their visual field, literally out of their space. Replace them with hopeful, happy, and inspirational drawings, photos, or memories.

Case study: Child

Elliot is 10 years old. He was referred for anxiety and panic disorder after being a passenger in a car accident. He was not physically injured.

The clinician introduced Elliot to the Old Things tool. Elliot stated that he had several items in his room that still reminded him of the car accident, the most difficult one being his backpack. He remembered his backpack being thrown across the car. Elliot had not shared this with his parents, and he was now ready to share and to get a new backpack. In his room there is a photograph of

Positive Thinking

Elliot and his grandpa fishing, which is a fun and soothing memory for him. He also has a bear that his grandparents gave him. Even though he stated that he was too old for stuffed animals, he revealed that he slept with the bear from time to time as it helped him to feel secure, like he did when he was with his grandpa.

Case study: Adolescent

Karina is a 16-year-old who was referred for issues of anxiety. Her parents are in the military, and she recently had to move schools and States.

The clinician introduced Karina to the Old Things tool. Karina shared that she had many photographs and stuffed animals from her friends from around the country. She had moved multiple times, across the country and around the world. She shared that the photos of her friends were both comforting and sad at the same time. She missed them and continued to keep in contact with them. Her various stuffed animals provided her with comfort and soothing, especially the older ones from when she was a young child. She surrounded herself with uplifting quotations that she had found and taped to her mirror or hung in frames on her bedroom walls.

155

OUTSIDE OF YOU

VISUAL/VERBAL

Purpose

To help the child or adolescent strengthen their belief in a power outside of themselves.

What you will need

★ Only you

Activity

Ask the child or adolescent if they have a spiritual tradition, or believe in God, a higher power, the universe, etc. Ask how they strengthen their connection—do they pray, meditate, stargaze, etc.? Encourage their connection with the power outside of themselves. They can ask for help from their source, and get strength from these beliefs and traditions.

Case study: Child

Ana is a five-year-old who was referred after the sudden death of her mother.

The clinician introduced Ana to the Outside of You tool. Ana revealed that she believed in God and that her father and grandparents took her to the synagogue. Ana revealed that she knew her mother was okay and that she would see her again someday. This spiritual tradition was a great strength and comfort for Ana and her family.

Case study: Adolescent

Revere is a 14-year-old who was referred for depression. His father committed suicide when Revere was 12 years old.

The clinician introduced Revere to the Outside of You tool. Revere shared that he had both a spiritual tradition that provided him with comfort and active support from his church family. He further revealed that he also found great comfort in nature and in thinking about the vastness of the universe. On a family vacation he was able to look through an immensely powerful telescope, and what he viewed gave him comfort and hope.

TOMORROW IS A NEW DAY

VISUAL/VERBAL

Purpose

To remind the child or adolescent that although it sometimes feels as if they are stuck in the moment and like tomorrow will never come, it will.

What you will need

★ Only you

Activity

Discuss with the child or adolescent feelings of being stuck in the moment. Explain to them that tomorrow will come, and with it will come new opportunities for feeling different, thinking different, and ultimately healing and feeling better. It is already tomorrow in Australia!

Case study: Child

Kirsten is an 11-year-old who was referred due to her second removal from home due to neglect.

The clinician introduced Kirsten to the Tomorrow is a New Day tool. Kristen revealed that she felt like her mother would never get better. She had been angry with her mother for a long time. Kirsten had had to take care of her siblings when her mother was under the influence of drugs and alcohol. She further revealed that she had had to ask neighbors for food on multiple occasions.

Case study: Adolescent

Coran is a 17-year-old who was referred for school expulsion and running away from home.

The clinician introduced Coran to the Tomorrow Is a New Day tool. Coran revealed that it was always the same for him. Teachers at school, his mother, and his aunt all told him that he was becoming uncontrollable, and he was starting to feel hopeless. Coran stated that the only way he could see a new day would be for him to be able to get back to school to graduate and to get a technical degree or internship.

This was a good beginning for Coran.

STUCK IN THE MUCK

VISUAL/VERBAL

Purpose

For the child or adolescent to understand that it is easy to get stuck on thoughts, memories, or emotions, and for them to identify what it feels like to be stuck, and ways to get unstuck.

What you will need

★ Only you

Activity

Discuss the idea that when people get stuck in the muck, some people may feel physically tired and others may feel like they can't think of new thoughts and only have strong, old thoughts.

Ask the child or adolescent what they feel like when they are stuck in the muck. What have they done in the past to get themselves out of the muck? What could they do today?

Case study: Child

Daisy is a nine-year-old who was referred for issues of hitting and biting her adopted sister, aged two. One of the bites was on the child's face and required stitches.

The clinician introduced Daisy to the idea of the Stuck in the Muck tool to initiate conversations about being stuck in anger or rage with her sister. Daisy revealed that up to date the only thing that she did to get unstuck was to act out. The clinician and Daisy worked together to think of doable alternatives to acting out.

Case study: Adolescent

Jenna, a 16-year-old, was referred for issues of depression, anxiety, and panic attacks. She has also been recently diagnosed with diabetes.

The clinician met with Jenna and explained the Stuck in the Muck tool. Jenna revealed that she had had strong new thoughts that she could not stop about the diabetes. She also revealed that in the past, when she had depression and anxiety, she used meditation or talking to her best friend to help relieve the symptoms.

This was a great start as Jenna could also begin to use tools that had previously worked for her.

ROCKET SHIP

VISUAL/VERBAL

Purpose

To determine what the child or adolescent would like to change in their life circumstances.

What you will need

★ Only you

Activity

Talk with the child or adolescent about how fast rockets move. Discuss the difference in speed between a rocket, an airplane, a car, and walking. Ask the child or adolescent, if they could make the speediest or fastest change in any aspect of their life, what would it be?

Case study: Child

Harry is an 11-year-old who was referred due to him having to adjust to his mother being away from home at a temporary mental health residential care program.

Harry identified the need for his dad to quit his job. He further identified that if his dad quit his job, then he could spend more time with Harry and his siblings, and more time with his mother, whom he identified as needing help. It became apparent in a noticeably short time that Harry had been exposed to a great deal of his mother's mental health crises, as had his siblings.

Case study: Adolescent

Chelsea is a 14-year-old who was referred for stealing from a local store.

The clinician explained the Rocket Ship tool and Chelsea stated that there was so much that she wished she could change from the past. She further revealed that her parents had told her they were angry and ashamed of her.

This was a great beginning for Chelsea and the clinician.

ENERGY AND POWER

HANDS-ON

Purpose
To highlight strengths during difficult times for the child or adolescent.

What you will need

- ★ Large sheet of paper or cardboard
- ★ Paint
- ★ Markers or crayons

Activity
Ask the child or adolescent to create a list of occasions when they have demonstrated great energy or strength and power when they have encountered difficult times. They can write, draw, or paint these.

Case study: Child
Dai is a seven-year-old who was referred for issues of neglect.

The clinician explained the Energy and Power tool and Dai created a list that included time spent with extended family, eating regular meals, and feeling as though he had power through his ability to share thoughts, fears, and concerns that he had never shared before.

Case study: Adolescent
Maria is a 15-year-old who was referred for depression.

The clinician explained the Power and Energy tool to Maria.

Maria created a list that included writing poetry during episodes of depression, which helped her cope. When she reads the poetry later, she recognizes her talents and strength.

This tool helped Maria to recognize a strength, her use of language and writing of poetry, which enables her to have more energy and feel some pride at times.

COLOR SPLASH

HANDS-ON

Purpose

For the child or adolescent to learn how to use color to express their current feelings state.

What you will need

- ★ Finger paints
- ★ Paintbrushes
- ★ Poster board
- ★ Color wheel

Activity

Tell the child or adolescent that this project is about freedom of expression. They will be creating with paint an image of how they currently feel. Discuss how different colors may make us feel—blue may mean soothing or sad; red may mean angry or vibrant, etc. Work through the color wheel together to identify the different feelings associated with different colors.

Ask the child or adolescent to choose a color that best represents how they feel, and to use their hands or a paintbrush to paint it out. Encourage them to paint large and to take up as much space on the poster board as possible. Discuss the painting together.

Case study: Child

Bertie is a nine-year-old with autism. At school he has recently become argumentative and has been calling his peers names such as "stupid" and "dumb."

The clinician introduced Bertie to the Color Splash tool. Bertie painted using a paintbrush and the color black. He started exceedingly small, and with encouragement was able to paint "big." Bertie stated that he had recently felt like he did not have as many friends as he used to. He shared that it was difficult for him to wait for his peers to catch up with him, especially his friends, who he sometimes felt like he did not fit in with.

This tool allowed Bertie and the clinician to have a beginning conversation on ways to better engage with his peers and ways to cope with his frustration.

Case study: Adolescent

Miguel is a 15-year-old who was referred for physical violence with his mom, sister, and a police officer.

The clinician introduced Miguel to the Color Splash tool. Miguel appeared angry, but was unwilling to communicate. He grabbed the finger paint and poured red paint on the poster board. Miguel used his hands to move the paint quickly around the entire poster board. When he was done, he asked if he could use more color. He then added black, and with both hands traced the black paint throughout the poster board. When he was finished, he sighed.

Miguel appeared relieved to be able to let go of his feelings of betrayal and anger. He shared that the colors red and black represented anger and betrayal. He shared that he was incredibly angry with his mom and sister, and further, that he felt betrayed that his mom or sister had called the police on him.

This was a critical start to allowing Miguel to express and release a bit of his current feelings state of anger and betrayal.

NEW VISIONS

Purpose

To allow the child or adolescent to explore possible new ideas and behaviors they could participate in that are fun or creative.

What you will need

- ★ Paper
- ★ Markers or crayons

Activity

Provide the child or adolescent with some paper and markers or crayons. Explain that they have the opportunity to be creative—they can create a list of fun opportunities or behaviors to explore. Provide examples such as visiting the local museum or library, or learning a new language or instrument. They can take the list home as a reminder of their coping and creativity.

Case study: Child

Timothy is a 10-year-old who was referred for behavioral issues of aggression at home and at school after his father and brother had left the home.

The clinician introduced Timothy to the New Visions tool. Timothy stated that there were many things that he would like to do, but he did not know how he would be able to do them. He revealed that his mother frequently cried and that his aunt, who now lived with them, had stated many negative things about his father and brother. Timothy determined that he could walk to the local library and participate in summer activities there.

Case study: Adolescent

Parker is a 15-year-old who was referred for issues of depression and truancy.

The clinician introduced Parker to the New Visions tool. Parker revealed that she used to dream of traveling and doing many wonderful things; however, at this point she had been comparing herself and her family's resources with other peers at school. She felt sad that she was not able to go on vacations and to see other countries, like some of her peers. She attended a local high school where most students were either upper class or upper middle class. Parker revealed that she was able to continue to participate every summer at the water ski and boat club at the lake in her community. She said that she loved sailing, and, although her family did not have a boat, she could continue to learn with her friends.

This was a good beginning to opening up for Parker.

MOUNTAINS TO CLIMB OR JUNGLES TO EXPLORE

VISUAL/VERBAL

Purpose

To allow the child or adolescent to name difficult or frightening situations.

What you will need

- ★ Images of mountainous land that is rough and rocky and hard to pass and a jungle that is dark and full of vines and thick foliage, which makes it hard to pass through

Activity

As you show the images of the mountains to the child or adolescent, discuss how rough and difficult it may be to attempt to walk over the rocks and climb the mountain.

As you present the image of the jungle, discuss its darkness, the thickness of the foliage, and how difficult it may be to move through it.

Ask the child or adolescent about a time when it was difficult to move through, either currently or in the past.

Case study: Child

Jaxson is a nine-year-old who was referred for autism spectrum disorder issues and missing multiple days of school due to stomach aches.

The clinician introduced Jaxson to the Mountains to Climb or Jungles to Explore tool. Jaxson related to the mountainous image.

He shared that he felt fearful of other students who made fun of him, and that at times he would pretend he was sick to avoid confronting them at school, even though he liked school and was excelling in some classes.

This tool provided Jaxson with a wonderful way to express his fears and concerns.

Case study: Adolescent

Meana is a 14-year-old refugee. She was referred as a victim of incest and repeated sexual abuse by men in her community.

Meana was introduced to the Mountains to Climb or Jungles to Explore tool. Meana particularly identified with the jungle image. She revealed that she would stay up at night, listening for noises, and looking for people in the shadows who wanted to harm her. She further revealed that she felt safe in her current home, but she was hypervigilant, scanning the environment for threats.

This was a wonderful beginning for Meana to open up about her trauma and current safety.

MONSTERS

HANDS-ON

Purpose
To enable the child or adolescent to describe people they are afraid of or feel unsafe around.

What you will need

★ Paper

★ Paint

★ Paintbrushes

Activity
Ask the child or adolescent to paint several monsters on the paper provided. Ask them to name or identify the scary people that the monsters represent.

Case study: Child

Willow is a seven-year-old who was referred for social withdrawal in second grade.

The clinician introduced Willow to the Monsters tool. Willow painted four monsters. She identified these as three friends from school and one of her siblings. Willow has been treated for a disease that caused a disfigurement to a portion of her face. She revealed that her closest friends at school had joined in with a group of peers to name-call and make fun of her scarring. She further revealed that one of her siblings had joined in this name-calling with her peer group at school.

This was a good beginning for Willow. She has overcome

many adversities, and her school and family were unaware of the bullying.

Case study: Adolescent

Christopher is a 13-year-old who was referred for issues of bullying and incivility.

The clinician introduced Christopher to the Monsters tool. Christopher reacted strongly by asking if he should draw himself. Christopher revealed that he had been a victim of bullying. He further revealed that he felt that if he was an aggressor, others would not attempt to bully him. Christopher did settle down and painted one monster, which he identified as a teacher who, in a previous grade, had bullied and belittled him in front of his peers on numerous occasions.

This tool helped the clinician to gain an understanding of Christopher's own self-identity as sometimes a monster, as well as to learn about Christopher's personal experience, which had not been noted to date.

SEASONS

HANDS-ON

Purpose

To help the child or adolescent identify what kinds of things they would normally be doing during this time of year, and to facilitate engagement in these activities as a form of soothing, comfort, and familiarity.

What you will need

- ★ An image of whatever season you are currently in
- ★ Paper
- ★ Gel pens
- ★ Stickers, such as stars or a thumbs-up sign
- ★ Marker

Activity

Share with the child or adolescent the image of the season you are currently in. Ask what types of things they would normally be doing during this time of year, such as getting ready for school, being in summer camp, sledding, etc.

Write the list together with the gel pens. Have the child or adolescent place stickers next to the activities that they enjoy the most or that provide them with the most comfort.

Use the marker to circle one or two of the activities that they could engage in straightaway.

Case study: Child

Otto is a six-year-old who was referred due to acting-out behaviors at home. His family has recently moved from abroad.

The clinician introduced Otto to the Seasons tool. Otto was able to readily identify the many things he did "at home." He shared going to camp with his cousins, having sleepovers with his cousins at his home and his cousins' home, and spending time with his grandpa and grandma. He was very distressed about not knowing how to communicate or what to expect. He had been attending his school since he was three, along with his cousins. He missed them and his family.

This was a great beginning for Otto. He was able to articulate the many things he enjoyed, but also the disconnect with not knowing what to expect in another country, and with both of his parents being preoccupied with their work.

Case study: Adolescent

Vince is a 13-year-old who was referred for internet addiction and loss of connection with his close local friends.

The clinician introduced Vince to the Seasons tool. Vince shared that he was upset that people believed he was addicted to the internet. The clinician asked Vince what he would engage in outside of the internet last summer. Vince revealed that last summer was different as his family would spend weekends at a summer home, where he would swim, hike, and camp out with his cousins or his friends. Vince stated that was no longer interested in accompanying his parents to the summer home or engaging with his cousins or his friends outside of gaming. Vince revealed that if he was allowed to stay on the internet all day long, he would.

This was a good opening conversation about how involved Vince was with the internet and gaming, and how isolated he had become.

RELEASE GUILT

HANDS-ON

Purpose
To allow the child or adolescent to identify and let go of feelings of guilt.

What you will need

- ★ Paper
- ★ Pen

Activity
Discuss the issue of guilt, and allow the child or adolescent to share issues for which they are harboring feelings of guilt. Encourage them to write out their feelings to discuss and help rid themselves of these feelings.

Case study: Child

Pilar is an 11-year-old who was referred for issues of grief after a change in guardianship, from her mother to her aunt.

The clinician introduced Pilar to the Release Guilt tool. Pilar shared that she suffered from much guilt. She had been placed in kinship care several times, and believed that on some level her actions or behaviors might, in some way, have led to her mother's loss of guardianship. Additionally, it was revealed that her mother had recently sent a letter to Pilar, saying how much she missed her. This caused further guilt and anguish for Pilar.

This tool allowed the clinician and Pilar to readily begin to address her guilt and suffering.

Case study: Adolescent

Ezra is a 16-year-old who was referred for grief after his mother died in a car accident in which he was involved.

The clinician introduced the Release Guilt tool to Ezra. Ezra immediately began to sob. He revealed that he had suffered from profound guilt since the death of his mother. Ezra shared ongoing family discord due to his acting-out behaviors. He had lost his driving privileges as punishment for bad choices and a bad attitude. He had been arguing with his mother at the time of the accident.

This tool allowed Ezra to share and move into a dialog regarding his guilt, trauma, and grief.

FEEL ALL OF YOUR FEELINGS

HANDS-ON

Purpose

To help the child or adolescent to describe their current feelings.

What you will need

- ★ Paper
- ★ Markers

Activity

Draw a pie chart for the child or adolescent and have them create sectors to show their feelings, and which feelings are most dominant.

Remind them that we do not have to judge our feelings, and we are entitled to have these feelings.

Read out the following script:

Sometimes unexpected and painful events occur, and we become untrusting of our own feelings. It is okay to feel and to feel the breadth of human emotion. Please do not forget as you are feeling all of your feelings to look for ALL, including the good, and begin to trust yourself—regain a sense of your self-responsibility and self-love. Even when the feelings overwhelm you, stop, take stock of yourself, your heart, and stop or slow the overwhelm, if you can. Breathe through it—you will come out the other side. Feel and let go, feel and let go, again and again, until you can let go completely for now and are free in this moment.

Case study: Child

Raina is a 10-year-old who was referred for night terrors and for sucking her thumb.

The clinician introduced Raina to the Feel All of Your Feelings tool. Raina and the clinician together created a list of feelings. They wrote them in the different-sized sectors to represent the amount of the emotion. Not unexpectedly, Raina's pie chart was almost all fear. She was, however, able to have some feelings of happiness when she was with her older sister, cousin, or friends.

This was a great start for Raina as she was able to begin the conversation surrounding her fear and thumb-sucking behavior, as she engaged in this behavior while talking about her feelings.

Case study: Adolescent

Clarise is a 13-year-old who was referred for sudden changes in her school grades and not engaging with her siblings or peers.

The clinician introduced Clarise to the Feel All of Your Feelings tool. Clarise quietly completed her pie chart. To her surprise she had many feelings of anger and distrust. It became apparent to the clinician and to Clarise that she was minimizing some of her feelings, and her inability to talk about or recognize those feelings increased her feelings of sadness and isolation.

This tool was helpful in getting quickly to the root of Clarise's feelings.

NARROW THINKING

HANDS-ON

Purpose

To help the child or adolescent shift from negative thinking to what is positive or working in their life.

What you will need

- ★ A cardboard tube such as from a paper towel
- ★ Paper
- ★ Pens or markers

Activity

Tell the child or adolescent to look through the cardboard tube. What do they see? Talk with the child or adolescent about how our vision may be limited, like looking through a tunnel—we can't see the wider perspective. Sometimes when we are overwhelmed by a situation, that is all we can think about. Sometimes our thoughts are primarily negative or harsh.

Ask the child or adolescent to share positives about themselves and their interactions with the world around them. Have them create a list to take home as a reminder to look for the positives.

Case study: Child

Allan is a 12-year-old who was referred for anxiety and acting out behaviors.

The clinician introduced Allan to the Narrow Thinking tool. Allan stated that lately he had been consumed with his parents arguing at home. It was hard for him to concentrate at times. He further revealed that he didn't know what kind of environment he would be coming home to daily. Many times, his parents would argue and throw things on the floor. One time he came home, and food and plants were spilled onto the floor. He was very frightened.

This tool was an excellent beginning for Allan to reveal his anxieties and fears and reasons for acting out.

Case study: Adolescent

Levi is a 15-year-old who was referred after witnessing his friend being hit by a car.

Levi reluctantly looked through the cardboard tube. He was able to identify that he was having tunnel vision and that all he could think about was his friend being in the accident. The clinician and Levi talked about how close he was to his friend and how both his friend's life and his own life had changed forever.

The clinician was able to move Levi into thinking about things he could still engage in with his friend. Even though his friend's physical state and mobility were different now, they could still participate in life. Levi agreed and stated that they had already been playing video games together and had watched some movies. He stated that the strength of the friendship had not changed.

This tool provided much needed information about the trauma that Levi experienced as well as reminders of the good times he could still have with his friend.

CARING FOR YOURSELF

HANDS-ON

Purpose

To identify ways the child or adolescent can self-soothe and care for themselves.

What you will need

- ★ An image of a plant or a real plant

- ★ Paper

- ★ Markers or crayons

Activity

Show the child or adolescent the plant.

Ask them what the plant needs to be healthy. Then ask, what do they need to stay healthy? Create a list of activities that they can do that are about self-care. What is something that they could do today?

Case study: Child

Ella is a 10-year-old who was referred after her family was evicted from public housing.

The clinician introduced Ella to the Caring for Yourself tool. Ella stated that it was hard to do the things that she usually liked to do to take care of herself, such as painting her nails or dancing in her bedroom. She was now located in temporary housing and she and her mother and sister were living in the same room, with bunk beds and a single bed. She had no privacy.

Ella was able to identify that at times she soothed or cared for herself by reading some of the books from the library in her building. She had also picked up some books and read them out loud to her younger sister, and she found these activities very calming.

This tool helped Ella to understand that she had been able to self-soothe and help her sister by reading to her.

Case study: Adolescent

Larry is a 16-year-old who was referred for anger and acting out on the school principal.

The clinician introduced Larry to the Caring for Yourself tool. Larry stated that he really didn't care about himself or what others thought of him. He shared that he had tried to get ahead in school, but he couldn't concentrate and had difficulty remembering things.

Together Larry and the clinician decided that it would be useful if Larry shared his difficulties so that he could get help. Larry shared that he was worried that his friends would make fun of him. He also recognized that they were already making fun of him for being behind in his schoolwork. Larry decided that the best way to take care of himself was to create a list of the issues that he needed help with, and to present them to his mom, teacher, and advisor at school.

CONNECTIONS

HANDS-ON

Purpose

To help the child or adolescent to find strategies for coping and understand that others have similar issues, thus providing hope.

What you will need

- ★ Paper
- ★ Pens or markers

Activity

Explain to the child or adolescent that when major issues or concerns happen in our lives, we may feel like we are the only ones going through them. Explain that many people all over the world have the same or similar issues, from homelessness to depression.

Ask them if they have ever helped their friends through difficulties. Were their difficulties the same as or different from those they have experienced themselves? Did they feel as though their friend was any less good as a person or less of a friend because of their issue?

With the child or adolescent, write out a list of similarities and connections that they may have with other people and ways of coping through the issues.

Case study: Child

Maeve is an 11-year-old who was referred for anxiety and difficulty making friends. She had recently moved and started a new school.

The clinician introduced Maeve to the Connections tool. Maeve revealed that she had many friends at her old school and felt like she was very different at the new school. Maeve remembered that when a new student came into her old school, everyone surrounded her and helped her out. Maeve stated that she had been the center of attention for a few days and then only two friends had helped her. The clinician and Maeve talked about one of the friends sharing that she had moved and understood the difficulty making friendships.

This was a great beginning tool as Maeve was able to identify that she did have friends and that one of her friends had had a similar experience to her.

Case study: Adolescent

Mia is a 17-year-old who was referred for issues of anxiety and depression. She had recently undergone knee surgery and was now out of the basketball season. All her friends and teammates were being scouted by colleges, and she was extremely discouraged.

The clinician introduced Mia to the Connections tool. The clinician shared that she had had a similar situation several years ago with another client. The other client had been able to gather videos from friends, family, and the coach to provide to potential scouts.

This tool enabled Mia to recognize that she was not alone, and that other options existed for her to move forward with her potential basketball career.

LEARN TO BECOME QUIET

HANDS-ON

Purpose
To enable the child or adolescent to self-soothe and calm.

What you will need

- ★ Quiet music or nature sounds

- ★ Paper

- ★ Pens or markers

Activity
Share with the child or adolescent the intention of helping them to learn to self-soothe.

While listening to the music or nature sounds, ask the child to recall things that help them to feel calm or safe, and to write these down.

Case study: Child
Moranda is a seven-year-old who was referred for adjustment issues with anxiety due to loss of a parent.

The clinician introduced Moranda to the Learn to Become Quiet tool. Moranda was able to immediately identify that her maternal grandmother and her aunt provided her with great peace. She enjoyed snuggling up and reading with her aunt and making cookies with her grandmother. Moranda also listed her pet dog and her grandmother's two birds as calming for her.

Case study: Adolescent

Lilibet is a 17-year-old who was referred for issues of anxiety that have manifested in her picking at her skin and pulling out her eyebrows and eyelashes—trichotillomania.

The clinician introduced Lilibet to the Learn to Become Quiet tool. Lilibet revealed that she had a lot of anxiety surrounding her senior year in high school. She was worried that she would not get into college or that she would not be able to afford college. She had talked with her mother and father multiple times, and revealed that she felt comforted and tended to calm down after talking with them. Lilibet also realized that when she took warm baths and took time during her day and did not feel rushed, she was able to be more calm and relaxed.

RECOGNIZE STOP SIGNS

HANDS-ON

Purpose

To help children and adolescents identify internal cues that signal they need to stop and reassess the current situation and their behaviors.

What you will need

- ★ Roll-out drawing paper or large poster boards taped together

- ★ Thick marker

- ★ Band-Aids

- ★ Stickers, such as lightning bolts, fire or flames, water or tears, clenched hands or fists, etc.

Activity

Ask the child or adolescent to choose if they would like to draw the outline of themselves or if they would prefer their parent/guardian trace them on the roll-out drawing paper or poster boards.

Ask the child or adolescent to place the various stickers or Band-Aids where they feel they experience them in their body, and what they mean—for example, placing the fists on their hands may mean they are angry and/or are ready to fight, verbally or physically.

Case study: Child

Ramos is a 10-year-old who was referred for vandalizing several lockers in the school as well as pushing and injuring two children in first grade.

The clinician introduced Ramos to the Recognize Stop Signs tool. Ramos asked his mother to draw his outline on the paper. He seemed to enjoy it and laughed. He said it tickled him. Ramos stuck some Band-Aids on his stomach and his mouth. He revealed that his stomach hurt, and he felt like throwing up when he was upset. He said that the children's lockers that he had vandalized deserved it, as did the first graders he had pushed, as they were family members of a boy who had been involved in getting Ramos's brother permanently expelled from school.

Case study: Adolescent

Kevin is a 16-year-old who was referred for combative behavior, which ultimately ended in him pushing his teacher and his mother.

The clinician introduced Kevin to the Recognize Stop Signs tool. Kevin was happy to create his own outline. He readily used stickers representing fists, an angry face, steam coming out of his ears, a Band-Aid on his heart and one on his head, and lightning bolt stickers all around his body. Kevin revealed ongoing feelings of anger that he could not control. He had attempted to talk with numerous adults and felt like no one was listening. He was able to identify feelings of tension in his body, his heart racing, and shallow breathing. He also noted that before his angry behaviors he would have a feeling of energy, like a spark of adrenaline. Kevin was able to identify these signs that could help him to slow down, stop, and evaluate his state before doing something destructive.

JUMBLED

HANDS-ON

Purpose

To help the child or adolescent clarify jumbled thoughts or feelings.

What you will need

★ Poster board or a recycled pizza box

★ Thick markers

Activity

Share with the child or adolescent that jumbled thoughts and feelings may take up a lot of time and energy in our day-to-day being. Ask them what thoughts or feelings are jumbled up for them. Write a list of the thoughts or feelings on poster board or a pizza box.

Try to notice if there is a pattern, and determine if there may be one or two things that the child or adolescent can do immediately to move in the direction of corrective action.

Case study: Child

Indie is a 12-year-old who was referred for depression.

The clinician introduced Indie to the Jumbled tool. Indie created a list of 10 issues and feelings that were jumbled up in her mind. She was able to identify a pattern of general depression and hopelessness, particularly surrounding her parents' divorce.

This was a good beginning to opening up for Indie.

Case study: Adolescent

Tyrell is a 16-year-old who was referred for ongoing acting-out behaviors in school.

The clinician introduced Tyrell to the Jumbled tool. Tyrell stated that he was so bound up in anger that this was all he could think about or feel.

This was a great beginning for Tyrell as he was able to open up about the dominant feeling of anger that was overwhelming him.

SUPERSTRENGTH

HANDS-ON

Purpose

To help the child and adolescent be creative and ultimately look at any needs they may have in terms of power and safety.

What you will need

* ★ Images of world record holders

* ★ Paper

* ★ Markers

Activity

Share the images of the different records that individuals have set, from growing the largest pumpkin to benching the most weights. Ask the child or adolescent to identify what superstrength they have, and how it has propelled them ahead.

Case study: Child

Juan is a 10-year-old who was referred due to adjustment issues as he has recently migrated to the US from Mexico.

The clinician introduced Juan to the Superstrength tool. Juan identified that he was able to read at such a quick speed that he had excelled in school. In addition, he had become invaluable to his family, as he was able to help them by interpreting information quickly. Juan felt proud and happy that he was able to help his family adapt to their new country.

Case study: Adolescent

Leila is a 13-year-old who was referred for sudden issues of with-drawal and social isolation.

The clinician introduced Leila to the Superstrength tool. Leila stated that there were several superstrengths that she used to have in middle school; now that she was in high school, however, she was not the best academically. The most important super-strengths that she had were her reading ability and her interest in science.

This was a good beginning for Leila as she had forgotten that she was still a good student; she was just not ready for all the competition in high school.

FUN TIMES

HANDS-ON

Purpose

To help the child or adolescent focus on something other than trauma. These real-life memories can provide an emotional break.

What you will need

- ★ Poster paper

- ★ Markers or crayons

Activity

Together with the child or adolescent, create a list of fun memories that they have experienced with family and friends.

Case study: Child

Aruna is a seven-year-old who was referred after the sudden death of her paternal grandmother, whom she lived with.

The clinician explained the Fun Times tool. Aruna created a list of things that she had done with her grandmother: cooking, sewing, and especially singing. Her grandmother had also spent many times with her when she had not felt well and her parents were at work. She also listed several family members whom she was close to and whom her grandmother was close to as well. These individuals had many memories and joy for Aruna.

Case study: Adolescent

Arthur is a 15-year-old who was referred due to anxiety surrounding his potential move across country due to his father's job relocation.

The clinician introduced Arthur to the Fun Times tool. Arthur shared that he had many fun memories. He listed his family, friends, and especially his cousins. This tool was an eye-opener for Arthur as two of his cousins live in the same town that he may be relocating to.

This tool not only helped Arthur to remember all of his good memories; it also allowed him to have some peace if he did have to move.

LIGHTHEARTED

HANDS-ON

Purpose

For the child or adolescent to change emotional states by remembering lighter or less stress-filled times, and to provide hope for better times in the future.

What you will need

- ★ Poster board
- ★ Markers or crayons

Activity

Share with the child or adolescent that they will be creating a list of memories that are neutral or less stressful than what they are currently experiencing.

Case study: Child

Jacob is a 10-year-old who was referred for issues of anxiety and depression following his parents' separation.

The clinician shared with Jacob the Lighthearted tool. Jacob was able to recall many memories that were neutral or happy. He revealed that he was concerned that he may not see his dad as frequently, as his mum had told him that she hoped he didn't.

This tool was critical in helping the clinician to assess quickly the nature of Jacob's distress and begin to move forward with coping.

Case study: Adolescent

Marion is a 16-year-old who was referred for anxiety due to home difficulties.

The clinician introduced the Lighthearted tool to Marion. Marion revealed that it was difficult to remember lighthearted or neutral memories as most of her life her parents had been in and out of jail, and she had lived in multiple households with multiple family members. Marion was eventually able to talk about several family members whom she had resided with over time and currently lives with, whom she has watched movies with and talked about the future with. This provided her with a sense of security. She did not want to have to move to another household again.

This tool was able to get to the root causes of Marion's difficulties and anxiety and help her and her family to recognize the impact the changing of households had had on Marion.

GET QUIET, GET CALM

VISUAL/VERBAL

Purpose

For the child or adolescent to learn how to relax or feel calm.

What you will need

★ Only you

Activity

Ask the child or adolescent to simply notice themselves in the room being present with you. Ask them to focus on one item with you, and to notice any changes in their body in terms of their relaxation response.

Case study: Child

Felicia is an 11-year-old who was referred for anxiety of an unknown origin.

The clinician introduced Felicia to the Get Quiet, Get Calm tool. Together Felicia and the clinician focused on a vase of black and yellow sunflowers. As they focused together the clinician asked Felicia if she could notice herself calming down. Felicia was able to relax. She stated that she had not felt that calm for a long time. The clinician reinforced that Felicia could use this tool with any object at home or at school.

Case study: Adolescent

Nancy is a 16-year-old who was referred for anxiety after being a passenger in a car accident. She was not injured, and neither was anyone else.

The clinician introduced Nancy to the Get Quiet, Get Calm tool. Nancy revealed that she felt anxious, not only in cars, but everywhere. Together they focused on a vase of sunflowers. Nancy revealed that it was hard for her to stay focused. Every time she tried to calm down, images of car accidents filled her mind.

This was a great beginning to opening up for Nancy.

WHEN BAD FEELINGS COME

VISUAL/VERBAL

Purpose

For the child or adolescent to be able to determine healthy ways of alleviating anxiety.

What you will need

★ Only you

Activity

Ask the child or adolescent to identify what they currently do when bad feelings arise. Whom do they go to for help? What do they tell themselves to calm down? How do they self-soothe?

Case study: Child

Kelly is a six-year-old who was referred for issues of child neglect and abandonment. She currently lives with her biological aunt.

The clinician introduced Kelly to the When Bad Feelings Come tool. Kelly revealed that she sought out her aunt for comfort, and sometimes slept with her aunt because she was worried that her aunt may disappear. Kelly further revealed that she has a blanket and a robe that came from her mother's home that she could cuddle, which helped her to feel safe.

Case study: Adolescent

Harriet is a 16-year-old who was referred for issues of anxiety and picking behavior. Harriet will be graduating from high school when she is 17.

The clinician introduced Harriet to the When Bad Feelings

Come tool. Harriet revealed that for over a year her worries had been escalating as she was thinking about what to do for college. Harriet is the only person in the family to go to college. Harriet revealed that she used to use reading and writing poetry as her way of coping, but that lately this had not happened. She agreed to start her journaling and poetry writing again. She also decided that she would carry a small notebook with her and write about her feelings instead of picking.

WHAT KIND OF MUSIC ARE YOU TODAY?

VISUAL/VERBAL

Purpose

To help the child or adolescent understand and identify their feelings.

What you will need

- ★ Recordings of different genres of music

Activity

Explain the notion of the different types of music and how some music may make us feel relaxed while other music may make us feel sad, energetic, or happy, for example. Play several different types of music for the child or adolescent, and ask which type they identify with and what the emotion associated with it is. Sometimes they may choose more than one type of music.

Case study: Child

Erasmus is a nine-year-old who was referred for fighting behaviors at home and at school.

The clinician introduced Erasmus to the What Kind of Music Are You Today? tool. The clinician played different types of music and Erasmus identified two types of energetic music that made him feel like fighting, and more sad music that he identified with due to his own sadness. Erasmus shared that his older brother was in jail, and that he was very angry as many people at school made fun of him and his family, and he was also sad as he did not know when his brother would return. This was the second time that his brother had been incarcerated.

Case study: Adolescent

Eric is a 17-year-old who was referred for issues of defiance, both at home and at school. He has also been on probation two times this year due to inappropriate language with peers and teachers.

The clinician introduced Eric to the What Kind of Music Are You Today? tool. Eric readily identified that the music he wanted and needed was angry and energetic. Eric revealed that he feels angry that his family is so involved in their own personal dramas that they do not have the time to understand his issues.

CHANGING HATS

HANDS-ON

Purpose

To teach the child or adolescent how to move from one situation to another with a smooth transition.

What you will need

- ★ Different types of hat, such as a snow hat, baseball cap, hockey mask, etc.

Activity

Present the different hats to the child or adolescent. Discuss the different uses for each hat, and how we may use more than one during a day. Ask them how many transitions they have had or are having and what they feel like.

Case study: Child

Griffin is an eight-year-old who was referred for a return to more clingy and childlike behaviors. Griffin's parents have recently divorced.

The clinician shared with Griffin the Changing Hats tool. Griffin identified the many different types of hat that people may have to wear in a day. Griffin shared that the hats that he must wear at his mom's and dad's homes are very different. The divorce and subsequent transitions are new for Griffin.

Case study: Adolescent

Howie is a 13-year-old who was referred after his mom relapsed. He is now living with his aunt.

The clinician shared the Changing Hats tool with Howie. Howie was able to identify with all the different changes and transitions that must occur for him daily. He revealed that not only were his aunt's house rules different than his mom's, but that his aunt was threatening to send him to a group home if he did not cooperate with her rules. Howie stated that his aunt was unwilling to talk about his mom's relapse.

GARDEN GNOMES

HANDS-ON

Purpose

To create some energetic, uplifting, and silly moments within a discussion.

What you will need

- ★ A set of silly-looking gnomes, or photos of silly-looking gnomes, or funny/silly images of your choice

Activity

Explain to the child or adolescent that the purpose of this activity is to let loose and be silly, and have some fun and a laugh. Share the images of the gnomes or other funny or silly images of your choice. See if any of them can elicit a moment of silliness, happiness, or lightheartedness in the child or adolescent.

Case study: Child

Jacob is a four-year-old who was referred for a check-in as he has officially been adopted by his foster family.

The clinician introduced Jacob to the Garden Gnomes tool. Jacob laughed and grabbed one of the tiny gnomes, stating that his mom had one like this in the backyard, in the hole of a tree. Jacob loves gnomes—his mom read him a book about them and how they live in hollow trees.

Case study: Adolescent

Christie is a 15-year-old who recently moved from a group home into a foster family.

The clinician introduced Christie to the Garden Gnomes tool by showing some silly photos of garden gnomes in surprise spots around a home and office building. Christie revealed that it was nice to think about lighthearted things. She needed a break from her worries. She revealed that she wanted to stay with her new foster family, and did not want to go back to the group home.

This was a great beginning for Christie.

VOLCANO

VISUAL/VERBAL

Purpose

To teach the child or adolescent that anger is an emotion that we all have, but it is how we express it that is important.

What you will need

★ A photo or short video of a volcano erupting

Activity

Present the child or adolescent with the photo or short video of a volcano erupting. Ask them about what they do with angry feelings.

Case study: Child

Tilly is a seven-year-old who was referred for issues of physical abuse.

The clinician introduced Tilly to the Volcano tool. Tilly immediately stated that she felt just like a volcano bursting. She was bursting with anger because of what had happened to her and her siblings. Tilly revealed that at times she got so angry that she would throw herself on the floor and scream.

This was a great beginning for Tilly as she was able to talk about her very volatile feelings.

Case study: Adolescent

Evette is a 16-year-old who was referred due to truancy issues.

The clinician introduced Evette to the Volcano tool. Evette revealed that when she felt like she could not take any more stressors at home, she would erupt with anger and rage. As a punishment she refused to go to school for her grandmother, and many times she would make her sister miss the school bus.

This was a good beginning for Evette as she was able to start to identify the many stressors that she was having difficulty identifying at home.

BUBBLES

HANDS-ON

Purpose

To determine what thoughts are coming into the child's or adolescent's mind, quickly and unhindered.

What you will need

- ★ Bubbles

- ★ A sheet of paper with the outline of five bubbles drawn on it

- ★ Pens or crayons

Activity

Allow the child or adolescent to blow bubbles. Notice how different they are—some are small, some are large, some last longer than others. Ask the child or adolescent to write down in the five bubbles what their current thoughts are.

Case study: Child

Mark is a nine-year-old who was recently referred for pushing his teacher.

The clinician introduced Mark to the Bubbles tool. Mark played with the bubbles for a few minutes and identified several thoughts. The most concerning thought that he wrote in one of his bubbles was that he hates his teacher.

This was an excellent opening for the clinician and Mark to take the next steps in his anger towards his teacher.

Case study: Adolescent

Courtney is a 13-year-old who was referred for issues around grief after the loss of her dog.

The clinician introduced Courtney to the Bubbles tool. Courtney blew several bubbles and started to write in the bubble outlines. She shared that her dog was very important to her, as when her father had to leave for extended periods in the military, her dog was her comfort and her best friend. She further revealed that her father always told her when he was leaving that the dog was always there and loving her.

This was a great beginning for Courtney to begin to work on the grief for her dog and transitions when her dad was away from home.

I AM _____

VISUAL/VERBAL

Purpose

To allow the child or adolescent to start wherever they need to start.

What you will need

★ A sheet of paper with the words "I Am _____" printed on it

Activity

Discuss with the child or adolescent that they can start wherever they need to start. Today, they can simply fill in the statement "I Am _____."

Case study: Child

Amy is a 10-year-old who was referred for anxiety after being bullied.

The clinician introduced Amy to the I Am _____ tool. Amy immediately completed the "I Am" statement with the word "SCARED."

This was a great beginning for Amy as she was able to open up and begin to share.

Case study: Adolescent

Juanita is a 15-year-old who was referred for sadness and anger. She was recently caught shoplifting.

The clinician introduced Juanita to the I Am _____ tool. Juanita identified that she was ashamed. She revealed that her family was also very embarrassed by her behavior.

FOUNTAIN: WHAT IS BURSTING FORTH?

VISUAL/VERBAL

Purpose

To allow the child or adolescent to express strong emotions.

What you will need

★ A photo of a fountain with a large spray of water

★ An outline of a fountain with water bursting out in a big display

★ Pens or crayons

Activity

Show the child or adolescent the photo of the fountain with the water spraying out. Talk about the pressure that must accumulate in the fountain for the water to press through. Ask them to write in the outline of the fountain what emotions feel like they are bursting out or need to come out.

Case study: Child

Eli is a five-year-old who was referred after numerous incidents of crying and trying to hide at school.

The clinician introduced Eli to the Fountain: What Is Bursting Forth? tool. Eli drew a picture of two individuals physically fighting. He revealed that the individuals who were fighting were his parents. He also drew a picture of himself with tears falling down his face.

This tool was especially helpful as it allowed Eli to convey what was going on in his home and how it was impacting him.

Case study: Adolescent

Christine is a 14-year-old who was referred for spitting on a class-mate and lowering grades.

The clinician introduced Christine to the Fountain: What Is Bursting Forth? tool. Christine admitted that she had been so angry that she spat on her classmate. She stated that she had been boiling over with anger over the past several months. This individual and some of her friends had been bullying Christine and making derogatory statements about her family's financial condition. She revealed that they had made fun of her clothes, her shoes, and even the fact that she was on the hot lunch program. They knew she received a free lunch. Finally, Christine revealed that she wasn't sure if she wanted to continue to attend this school. Christine attends a private school on a tuition waiver.

This was a great beginning for Christine to be able to talk about many issues that have had a significant negative impact on her day-to-day school experience.

INDEX

index page